ANXIETY into ENERGY

ANXIETY into ENERGY

Victor Pease

HAWTHORN/DUTTON // NEW YORK

To my son Brad

Published in the United States by Elsevier-Dutton Publishing Co., Inc.,
2 Park Avenue, New York, N.Y. 10016

Library of Congress Cataloging in Publication Data

Pease, Victor.
  Anxiety into energy.

  Includes index.
  1. Stress (Psychology) 2. Anxiety. 3. Vitality.
I. Title.
BF575.S75P4 1981   158'.1   80–22788

ISBN: 0–8015–0335–3

Published simultaneously in Canada by
Clarke, Irwin & Company
Limited, Toronto and Vancouver

Designed by Mary Gale Moyes

10 9 8 7 6 5 4 3 2 1

First Edition

CONTENTS

PREFACE

Stress is something that we all experience. We must have stress to live. I have written this book to help you use your stress response to its fullest advantage. For many years, I have been working with people who have had tension problems. In their attempts to survive the pressures in their lives, they have allowed their stress energy to be transformed into tension and anxiety. Psychological and physical disorders are possible consequences.

Unfortunately we are only too aware of the unhealthy side of stress. We are most often told that it is to be avoided at all costs. We are meditating, medicating, jogging, and hot tubbing to prevent stress from overtaking us. The truth of the matter is that stress can be good for you if you can learn how to manage and use it.

This book will help you to use stress to feel better and to perform more effectively. You will learn how to generate stress energy and how to divert stress from producing ten· sion and anxiety. I have divided the book into two parts: Part I discusses some of the misconceptions surrounding stress and covers information to help you raise your awareness of how stress affects you; Part II offers a number of skills to help turn anxiety into energy. You may choose those skills that are appropriate for your personality and circumstances.

Your tasks will be to spend some time getting in touch with your physical and psychological stress responses, to select stress skills that are appropriate for you, and to *practice* them. I emphasize the word *practice*. It takes us years to acquire our stress-reaction patterns. They are not going to be changed overnight.

Learning how to relax does not give you the benefit of using stress, but it is an important first step. Sometimes it is necessary to increase stress not only for better performance but also to feel better. Several techniques are offered to you in this book because no one technique works for all. You can choose what is best for you. Learn to stop stress from becoming tension and anxiety. Use its energy to enjoy work and play.

ACKNOWLEDGMENTS

I owe a great deal of thanks to my editor, Constance Schrader. Her kindness and guidance helped make writing this book a pleasure, not a chore.

I was fortunate enough to have William "Pat" O'Mara as a partner and friend to use as a sounding board for my ideas. Carolyn Gould skillfully eliminated the stressors of typing and correcting the manuscript.

Finally I am indebted to the Management Institute of the School of Management of Clarkson College and the many other organizations for sponsoring so many of my stress-management seminars. The sharing of personal experiences and feelings by the many seminar participants was of great value to me. Special thanks are due to them.

1: BECOMING AWARE OF STRESS

1: THE NATURE OF STRESS

"I was driving to work on a Thursday morning. I had to meet with a labor relations man about our company's contract. We had been haggling for months on details and were ready to sign an agreement. I felt pretty well—had been having some trouble sleeping and felt tense, but that is part of the job. As I was driving, my face felt hot, but I had felt that way before, especially when I was under the gun. I also felt a little burning sensation in my stomach, but I had that every day. I went into the office to pick up the contracts and my notes. I felt a little pain in my left arm and chest. I sat down at my desk. The sweat began to roll off my face. My arm began to feel numb. My chest felt as if it were being crushed. I buzzed my secretary. She took one look at me, told me to lie down on the couch, and called an ambulance. Later at the hospital I heard what I didn't want to hear—heart attack. I couldn't believe it. I spent three weeks in the hospital and two months at home. I went back to the office, half days at first—then back to full time. After I went back, I realized how hectic everything was. There was nothing but constant bickering and haggling. Some of my upper management people fought all of the time. I was the only one who could keep them from killing one another. Well, what I want to tell you is that you would think that I had learned something from that first heart attack. But I didn't. I had another one two years later under almost identical conditions. The second time I knew what it was and went right to the hospital. The doctor said that it was not as bad as the first time. I was lucky.

Now let me tell you something else. Don't tell me that stress doesn't cause heart attacks. I had both of mine during two very stressful situations. I know that diet and exercise are important, but the tension of my job is killing me. I'm the top man. The place can't run without me, but my job is killing me. What am I going to do?"

I wish that I could tell you that cases like the one above are rare, but they are not. I *can* tell you that there is a happy ending.

The subject of that case is doing well. He has learned to manage his tension. During a stress-management seminar he learned about the physiology, psychology, and organizational aspects of stress. He developed a stress-management program for himself. He went back to work and delegated responsibility and authority to his top management teams. The company is doing well, and he is doing well.

It is difficult to explain to a person who has had a heart attack under those conditions that stress probably didn't cause it. Certainly, excessive stress might have been the final blow, but we just can't say that stress *caused* the attack. That is a misconception. Stress in this case might be the trigger that fires the bullet of years of living with excessive tension, anxiety, poor diet, inadequate exercise, smoking, and other kinds of self-abuse. What I am talking about is changing lifestyles. *Lifestyling* is a current buzz word that often triggers the response, "I don't have time for that." If that is your response, treat it as a warning sign. Concern over time, especially not having enough time, is a signal of a fast-paced life. This book is not a lot of words about slowing down. It is a book about using your energy in ways that increase your efficiency and effectiveness. The principles by which you can do that are not based upon philosophical advice but soundly established and tested principles of learning and problem solving. These principles are offered with the idea that you can choose those that fit your personality and circumstances. The time required will be a few minutes a day for a lifetime.

The first step in using the stress energy that you generate each day is to learn more about the nature of stress, some misconceptions and facts.

SOME MISCONCEPTIONS ABOUT STRESS

Complex topics are subject to confusion and misconception. Some misconceptions are so widely spread and firmly rooted that they are difficult to overcome. Stress is one of these topics. For example, do you believe that stress and tension are the same thing? That stress causes physical and mental illness? That it most commonly occurs in people who work under pressure and hampers their performance? Each of these statements is false.

MISCONCEPTION: STRESS AND TENSION ARE THE SAME

Part of the reason we have not learned to use stress as a positive adaptive force is because of our confusion of the terms *stress* and *tension.* Tension is a physiological stress reaction characterized by feelings of anxiety, worry, and pressure. While tension is most surely stress, it is only part, and the smallest part of the total stress response. It happens to be that part which we label as unpleasant. The following list presents common stress indicators made from the responses of 650 subjects. The indicators are rank ordered with the most frequently mentioned as number 1 and so forth.

1. Anxiety
2. Stomach distress
3. Heart rate
4. Increased activity
5. Mental confusion
6. Perspiration (palms)
7. Anger/frustration
8. Tremors
9. Depression
10. Eating (increases/decreases)
11. Biting fingernails
12. Rapid breathing
13. Loss of sleep (excess sleep)
14. Loss of self-confidence
15. Headache
16. Emotion: fear
17. Smoking (increases)

Not one subject gave a response that could be labeled favorable, that is, relating to adaptive stress. I wish to emphasize the word *label*, because the cognitive process of defining a situation (stressor) as pleasant or unpleasant partially determines whether the resulting stress response is adaptive or maladaptive. If the situation is labeled as pleasant, it is experienced as stimulating or exhilarating and is often followed by relaxation and positive psychological consequences. If it is labeled as unpleasant it is experienced as physical or psychological tension even though many of the stress indicators listed occur during pleasantly labeled experiences. Most of the stress that we experience is either neutral or positive. The preoccupation with the idea that stress is responsible for disease and suffering causes us to overlook its favorable aspects. Stress is a product of your interaction with your environment.

Our self-fulfilling prophecies are critical to success and health. Although adaptive stress and tension stress have similar if not identical physiological mechanisms, we must not confuse tension with stress. By doing this we begin labeling our natural bodily responses to stimulation as being tension. Worrying about worrying and feeling tense about tension are the results.

MISCONCEPTION: STRESS CAUSES DISEASE

The causal relationship between stress and disease has not clearly been established. After years of research we know that chronically excessive levels of stress may precipitate some heart attacks. Most of the statements relating stress to physical and mental disorders are based upon educated hunches, retrospective observations of stress and disease that are subject to errors of coincidence and observation. Animal studies show us that stress can debilitate and cause death. Nevertheless, experimental data showing that stress causes disease in humans are lacking.

The belief that stress causes disease often works its way into the guilt reactions of people who have had the experience of having a loved one suffer a heart attack. "Did I do something to cause the attack?" is a common question. They usually describe a specific incident they feel caused the attack. What they forget are the childhood diseases, heredity, current disease, overweight, excessive smoking, excessive drinking, irregular sleeping patterns, and poor physical condition of the person who has had an attack or has died. All of these factors plus more interact to produce coronary heart disease. Many heart attacks are a result of failure to learn healthy living patterns.

Experts in medicine and physiology vary in their opinions as to the importance of stress in causing disease. Some are conservative, doubting that stress itself can cause disease; others are certain that a major percentage of modern ailments are stress induced.

Some disorders that have been suspected as possibly having tension stress as a causal factor are:

Skin
Eczema—irritation of the skin
Neurodermatitis—chronic skin irritation; rash, lesions
Psoriasis—scaly patches of skin on chest, knees, and elbows
Hyperhidrosis—excessive perspiration
Acne—skin eruptions
Hives—allergic reaction; itchy welts or bumps on skin

Muscle
Backache—particularly lower back pain but also upper back
Arthritis—swollen and painful joints
Tension headaches—headache from muscle tension in neck or face
Muscle cramps—muscle spasms; excessive muscle tension
Myalgia—muscle pain

Respiratory
Hyperventilation—rapid breathing; overbreathing
Bronchial asthma—wheezing, respiratory distress
Hiccups—involuntary spasms of the diaphragm

Endocrine
Diabetes mellitus—abnormal insulin secretion, elevated blood glucose levels
Hyperthyroidism—overactivity of thyroid gland hormone production
Goiter—enlargement of thyroid gland; insufficient thyroid hormone production

Genitourinary

Impotence—inability to attain or sustain an erection satisfactory for intercourse

Dyspareunia—painful intercourse

Dysmenorrhea—painful menstruation, often later in life

Cardiovascular

Vascular spasms—constriction of blood vessels

Hypertension—elevated blood pressure, edema, kidney dysfunction

Migraine headache—throbbing headache, usually generalized; nausea

Raynaud's disease—constriction of small arteries, especially in fingers, nose, tongue

Paroxysmal tachycardia—irregular increases in heartbeat

Immunological; Allergic;
Blood and Lymphatic;
Gastrointestinal

Gastritis—chronic, excessive gas in the lower digestive tract

Gastric ulcer—ulceration of the mucous membrane of the stomach

Mucous colitis—colon inflammation, bowel disturbance

Constipation—infrequent bowel movement

Diarrhea—increase in fluidity, volume, and frequency of bowel movements

Heartburn—burning sensations in the stomach ·or esophagus

Mental illness and drug addiction are also often associated with attempts to cope with tension stress. To deny that tension stress is related to disease or intensifies existing disease is not wise. But to attribute a "killer" role to stress is equally unwise. The one thing that can be said is that our stress reactions are designed to promote our survival, not to end it.

MISCONCEPTION: STRESS
CAUSES MENTAL ILLNESS

For every person with a problem who has had a history of traumatic events, there is at least one who has experienced similar stressors but has not developed psychological problems. Heredity, past learning experiences, physical condition, and socioeconomic stressors interact in an almost incomprehensible way to cause disorders. To say that stress causes mental illness is tantamount to saying that life causes mental illness.

Some mental health experts estimate that one out of five people in the United States has some form of mental illness that requires treatment. This is an astoundingly high estimate of the incidence of mental illness. I believe that everyday problems, their tensions and anxieties, are being counted as mental illnesses requiring psychiatric help. More people need to learn to control more of their life rather than giving it away to professionals and drugs. Learning more about the psychology and physiology of stress is an important first step to help resolve tension problems.

Tension and anxiety are natural conditions of living. Sweaty palms, rapid breathing, accelerated heart rate are normal consequences of activity, not mental illness. The two great myths about mental illness are that stress causes it and that 20 percent of the people in this country require the services of mental health clinics.

MISCONCEPTION: STRESS CAN BE
ELIMINATED THROUGH THE USE OF DRUGS

Misperceptions and misunderstandings of physical and psychological stress responses lead to a desire for the quick "cure." Alcohol is used by many people to relieve tension, but prescribed antianxiety drugs take the lead in our attempts to cope with everyday pressures. Just to prove my point, in 1978 66 million prescriptions were written for the antianxiety drug Valium alone. Another 55 million prescriptions were written for other tranquilizers. Although the number of prescriptions of antianxiety drugs has been declining for the past few years, they are still overprescribed. Sadly, these drugs do not eliminate the causes of tension stress. Drugs do not solve problems; people solve problems.

Drugs can suppress the physical mechanisms underlying the stress response but do little to help the individual acquire new adaptive responses to effectively cope with the stressors active in their life. Actually, some of these drugs inhibit the adaptive-stress response that is needed for effective physical and psychological performance. If only those people with dangerously high levels of tension received drugs and were helped to learn new coping skills, then many drug problems would be eliminated. Unfortunately, that is not the case. Drug therapy tends to reinforce drug-taking behavior. In many cases the "cure" becomes another problem because of the addictive nature of the drug or the dependency nature of the consumer.

There is no question that certain psychoactive drugs, used properly, are beneficial in terms of alleviating human suffering and even in saving lives. The epidemic use of prescription drugs to reduce tension stress, however, may be creating more problems than are being solved. More research will have to be done to understand the benefits and risks of tranquilizer usage.

MISCONCEPTION: STRESS DISORDERS ARE MORE COMMONLY FOUND IN PEOPLE WHO WORK UNDER PRESSURE

Hundreds of corporations are investing resources in coronary prevention, meditation, biofeedback, and stress-management programs with the hope that executives and workers who work under pressure will not become mortality statistics. The cost of tension stress in American business is estimated to lie between $20 billion and $30 billion annually.

Numerous studies have attempted to determine which jobs are related to high levels of stress. A commonly employed indicator is the incidence of presumed stress-related diseases associated with various professions or employment. Long work hours, poor relations with supervisors, lack of job satisfaction are stressors for some workers. Although we might learn something about the physical demands of some kinds of work, these studies tell us very little about how people can learn to cope with job stressors.

The stress of making decisions. Many people believe that a top executive is especially prone to stress-associated diseases because of all the important decisions that must be made. Actually, the top executive mortality rate is much less than the average population. On the other hand, if individual executive case histories are considered, tension-stress disorders seem to be clearly related to the stressors of the job. I know a few executives who have experienced not one, but two heart attacks while negotiating important contracts or transactions. How can these two conflicting pieces of information about decision making be reconciled? Here is one very important answer to that question: People who thrive on stressful situations and escape physically and psychologically unscathed are those who perceive that they are in control rather than being controlled by their situation. Because of that perception, they label their stressors and stress reactions as being exciting and generally pleasant. They use their stress as energy for work, gain satisfaction out of their accomplishments, and know how to relax. For a while a classical animal experiment seemed to support the idea that decision making in itself was dangerous to health. That has been shown to be an incorrect interpretation as you will see by the following experiment.

Dr. Joseph V. Brady of the Johns Hopkins School of Medicine experimented with the effects of decision making upon the health of monkeys. The "executive" monkey had to press a lever to avoid an unsignaled shock every twenty seconds of a six-hour work shift followed by six hours of rest, twenty-four hours a day for several weeks. Another monkey went along for the ride. If the "executive" monkey did not press the lever in time, both monkeys received the shock. A problem with this experiment is that it is possible that the "executive" monkeys were selected for their job because they were "naturally" high-avoidance responders. They might well have had a constitutional predisposition to physical disorder under such severe stress conditions. New research indicates that "executive" monkeys do not develop ulcers as a consequence of making decisions. The subordinate monkeys, however, do. They are the ones who do not have any control over their fate. Finally, there is a serious question as to whether a monkey pressing a lever to avoid a shock is the same as an executive making a business decision.

Executives who are corporate chiefs as a group seem to be coping effectively with decision making. Either they reach the top because they know how to relax and use their stress or they have simply outsurvived everyone else. It is the rest of us who have to worry. Secretaries, laborers, plumbers, college professors, and housewives, to mention but a few, must make decisions daily that are just as important as a decision to merge a large corporation with another. The importance of a decision is defined by the person making it.

MISCONCEPTION: STRESS REDUCES PERFORMANCE AND PRODUCTIVITY

In addition to the mistaken view that decision making causes tension-stress disorders, there is the unfortunate notion that stress reduces effective performance and hence lowers productivity. An executive in one of my seminars said that she did not want to create stress in her employees by telling them what to do or criticizing their work. Another executive sitting across the table said that his problem was that his workers were so stress-free that they didn't get anything done.

The relationship between stress and performance on simple and complex tasks can be understood very clearly. Generally, increases in stress improve performance for simple tasks. Complex tasks and high levels of stress may lead to poor performance. Learning new skills and practice, however, can improve complex task performance under high levels of stress. Some of the greatest examples of human performance and precision are accomplished under intense levels of stress. Secretaries, musicians, athletes, homemakers, and surgeons, among others, learn to perform most effectively in stressful situations.

SOME FACTS ABOUT STRESS

Stress is the psychophysiological response of the body to a stressor that is labeled as pleasant or unpleasant by the individual experiencing it. The word *psychophysiological* is important and emphasizes the interrelationship between mind and body. A stressor is anything that places a demand on the body. The influence of physical agents upon the health of the body is well established. Psychosomatic medicine suggests that the mind is equally as powerful in affecting physical well-being as any disease, toxin, or physical injury. Difficulties in quantifying and predicting the impact of the psychological upon the physical have slowed acceptance of psychosomatic concepts.

The stress response itself can be nonspecific or specific. The nonspecific stress response has been extensively studied by Professor Hans Selye, Director of the Institute of Experimental Medicine and Surgery of the University of Montreal. In the nonspecific response, a stressor brings about a change which affects most parts of the body's stress systems. Other stress researchers such as psychologist Richard S.

Lazarus (1966) and endocrinologist John W. Mason (1971) have shown that the stress response can be very specific, involving only certain bodily systems and not others. When it comes down to talking about the consequences of our stress response, we are most often interested in the outcome. Is it beneficial or harmful? I prefer to use the terms adaptive stress to refer to the beneficial consequences of our stress response and maladaptive or tension stress to refer to the harmful ones.

The last part of my definition of stress involves the labeling of the perceived stress reaction and stressor as pleasant or unpleasant. Experience tells us that a stressor that creates maladaptive stress in one person might elicit adaptive stress in another. This apparent paradox is explained by the role learning plays in the acquisition of both specific and nonspecific stress responses to the various stressors we encounter in our lives. This is the ray of light in the darkness. Most maladaptive stress responses are learned and can be "unlearned" and replaced with beneficial responses.

Although the stress of being pleasantly surprised can be equivalent in intensity to stress generated during unpleasant conditions, it is those stressors that we label as unpleasant that most often result in maladaptive stress patterns. Once we label a stressor as unpleasant it can from that time on produce unpleasant consequences. Learning and the resulting labels we assign to stressors and our stress reactions are powerful forces in shaping the outcomes of our stress responses.

STRESS IS A NATURAL, CONSTRUCTIVE, AND ADAPTIVE RESPONSE

A most impressive example of the positive aspects of stress can be seen in the relationship between stress and performance. Athletes, opera singers, dancers, teachers, and many other professionals warm up or "psych up" before they perform. They are trying to develop an optimal level of stress to enhance their performance. This range of optimal stress is what I call the "stress window." When we find our stress window, we play better tennis, work more effectively, and even become better lovers. Through our stress window our physical performance is heightened. Senses and mind are sharpened as well. Emotions during these times are exhilarating. Stimulation coming from within the person or the environment is essential for achieving and maintaining optimal performance.

The body's stress response provides us with the physical energy necessary to work and play. The effectiveness of the immunoresponse of the body to ward off disease depends in part upon our stress response.

The energy to survive is derived from the stress response of the body. It is this one fact that compels us to reason that stress must be a constructive force in life. The destructive potential of excessive stress has been overemphasized to the point where there is some confusion as to how much stress is too much stress.

Even the amount and rate of information processed by our senses is dependent upon the general level of neural activation to stressors. Reduction of sensory stimulation has been shown to produce thought and perceptual distortion. Case studies of servicemen held in enemy concentration camps and experiments on sensory isolation, deprivation, and brainwashing indicate that restriction of sensory stimulation disorients and demoralizes some people. Those who create stimulation within their own mind are not as easily affected. Just as stimulation can be created by the mind in the absence of environmental stimulation, the mind can shut down its sensory channels and prevent information from being processed by the brain. This happens in everyday life to prevent informational overloading but in extreme cases is involved in some types of mental illness. Stimulation is necessary for physical and psychological health because it activates the stress response of the body.

THE RELATIONSHIP OF STRESS TO DISEASE

Because of the problems involved in quantifying and predicting the relationship of stress to specific diseases such as those of the cardiovascular system, not all experts agree on the role that stress plays in the disease process. Retrospective studies have established relationships between coronary heart disease and emotional events. Brief encounters with a stressor can produce dramatic short-term changes in blood pressure. In addition, chronic pressure changes occur in response to prolonged stressful situations. Heart attacks can be precipitated by excessive stress. Enough evidence is accumulating to confirm suspicions that tension stress is related to disease, but more research will have to be conducted to clarify this relationship.

STRESS PROMOTES GROWTH IN THE NERVOUS SYSTEM

When nerve cells die they are not replaced. Unlike other body cells, they do not reproduce. Studies comparing the brains of animals raised in enriched, stimulating environments, however, show that the brain increases its protein volume or grows in response to stimulation. Neural growth is undoubtedly dependent upon stimulation from the environment or stimulation from the internal activity of the individual. Neural growth or elaboration is very important for new learning, memory, and the compensation for the loss of nerve cells to natural cell death, toxins, or injury. Animals raised in sensory deprived environments, for example in complete darkness, show losses of neural tissue and visual perception that last for life. Monotony of environment has also been shown to induce perceptual disturbances and reasoning defects in humans for short periods of time. Humans need a certain optimal level of stimulation for healthy physical and psychological functioning.

STRESS CAN ELIMINATE BOREDOM

A monotonous environment may lead to boredom—but not necessarily. I've run into a few people who "kick and dip" for a living. All day long, they kick open a mold, fill a dipper with molten metal or plastic, and fill the mold. Many of these "kick and dippers" like their work. They are paid well and they "do a lot of thinking on the job." Many are not bored because they are able to keep mentally stimulated. In effect, they stress themselves. Boredom with a monotonous environment can lead to just as much anxiety as an environment loaded with threatening stressors. Boredom can arise from reducing environmental stimulation, but it can also come from the internal process of adaptation. Our nervous systems are designed to respond to change and to the novel aspects of our environment. Neural activity usually declines to repetitions of the same stimulus.

THE STRESS WINDOW

Heredity probably establishes potential upper physical exertion limits for the body. We are not doomed by heredity, however. Seldom does life demand that we push ourselves to the extremes of our physical limits. If we were subjected to such violent conditions, perhaps some of us would die from heart attack, some from kidney failure, some from ulcers, and so forth, because physical exhaustion might well actualize heredity's programmed upper limits. For most of us our general physical and psychological states are more important than heredity in meeting the stressors of everyday life. Each of us through our experience develops unique and complex patterns of responding to demands. We develop mental-sets, subjective ideas of what is too much, what is just right, and what is not enough to stimulate us. The variance in the stress-tolerance range of humans is great.

What is too much stress for one person may not be enough stimulation for someone else.

In every stress seminar that I have taught, the question always arises: "How do I know if I have too much stress?" By the end of the seminar, some have answered their own question; others are just beginning to find the answer. There is only one person who can define this range of stress tolerance for you, and that is yourself. Knowledge about stress and self-awareness are the first and most important steps in using your stress energy beneficially. Before going on to chapter 2, take the Tension-Stress Test that follows to learn more about your own tension level as a first step in self-awareness.

TENSION-STRESS TEST

	Many times a week	A few times a week	Rarely
I feel anger or frustration at home or work.	2	1	0
I feel tension or anxiety.	2	1	0
It is difficult to concentrate because of worrying about other things.	2	1	0
In conversation, I find myself finishing what the other person is about to say or interrupting.	2	1	0
My work involves deadlines/time pressures.	2	1	0
It is difficult for me to relax.	2	1	0
People at home/work make me tense.	2	1	0
I take tranquilizers (or other drugs) to relax or sleep.	2	1	0

TENSION-STRESS TEST (continued)

	Many times a week	A few times a week	Rarely
Thoughts race through my mind when I try to relax or sleep.	2	1	0
It is difficult to find enough time to relax.	2	1	0
I eat/drink/smoke in response to tension.	2	1	0
I have tension or migraine headaches.	2	1	0
I find it difficult to sleep or sleep is not refreshing.	2	1	0
I perspire during ordinary conversation or perspire excessively.	2	1	0
Annoyances tend to build up during the day.	2	1	0

TOTAL SCORE

SCORE	TENSION-STRESS LEVEL
18–30	Considerably above average
10–17	Above average
6–9	Average
0–5	Below average

The mean or average score on this test for eight hundred subjects is 7.7. A score of 12 or above would indicate that you might have a problem with tension stress.

This test was adapted from one developed originally by Dr. John W. Farquhar of the Stanford Heart Disease Prevention Program.

2: THE BODY AND STRESS

The body's stress response provides the energy to adapt to a changing environment. Nervous system pathways have been programmed over hundreds of thousands of years toward the single goal of survival. The stress response creates the energy to fight, to run away from danger, to work and play.

At birth each of us has from 10 to 12 billion nerve cells. Each nerve cell, called a *neuron,* has the properties of irritability and conductivity. Neurons respond to stimulation and conduct messages, called *nerve impulses.* Every behavior, thought, heartbeat, and hormone secretion is dependent upon the transmission of the neural message from one neuron to another. Each is a discrete functional unit, physically separated from its neighbor by a gap.

The area where two or more neurons come close to one another is called the *synapse.* Surprisingly, neurons communicate chemically rather than electrically. Each neuron secretes a minute quantity of a specialized chemical called a *neurotransmitter.* The diagram below presents a schematic diagram of a synapse. Neurotransmitters are released when

SYNAPSE

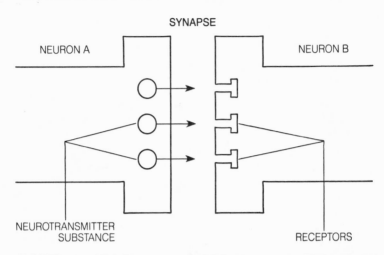

FIGURE 1 THE SYNAPSE AND SYNAPTIC TRANSMISSION

the neuron is stimulated. Synaptic vesicles are released from the terminal endings of one neuron and accepted by the neighboring neuron at special receptor sites. Receptor or binding sites only accept specific neurotransmitters that are of a certain organic structure. If enough transmitter is secreted, the receiving neuron will discharge and the process is repeated until the neural information reaches its destination in the brain, gland, muscle, or sense receptor.

Neurotransmitters are in delicate biological balance. Their relative concentrations underlie our physical activation levels. Too much of a certain transmitter may produce hyperactivity; too little, hypoactivity or physical depression. Nicotine, caffeine, tranquilizers, prescribed stimulants, and many other drugs affect the production of neurotransmitters. These drugs inhibit, block, or increase the production of neurotransmitters. Stress and relaxation also change transmitter levels. Approximately twenty major neurotransmitters have been identified and the search for new ones is frantically under way. The discovery of new transmitter systems will lead to the discovery of new drugs to affect them. The fact that some neurons accept only one transmitter has allowed the development of very specialized drugs that affect certain brain structures and not others.

The billions of neurons and their chemical transmitter substances ultimately control the body's stress response. As we confront a stimulus that we have labeled as a stressor or that places a physical demand upon us, enough neurons must release and accept just the right amount of neurotransmitter to control the organ systems that provide our energy. Neurons are arranged into nervous system structures that have specialized functions.

THE AUTONOMIC NERVOUS SYSTEM

The two general types of behavior important to the stress response are voluntary and involuntary. The voluntary nervous system is used to implement human intention. When we consciously wish to speak, remember something, or walk across the room, we are using the voluntary system. The involuntary, or autonomic nervous system, controls such physiological functions as breathing, heart rate, hormone secretion, the smooth muscle contractions of the intestines, and so forth. We now know that the involuntary nervous system is not as involuntary as we once thought. Autonomic nervous system functions can be controlled. Biofeedback is a learning process that uses the converted biosignals of the body to control voluntary and involuntary bodily functions. Many of the body's organs give off electrical signals when they function. Mechanical or electrical physiological responses can be measured with a recording device and translated into a sensory message that allows the subject to see or hear whether that activity is increasing or decreasing. Blood pressure, the volume of blood flow, muscle tension, and skin temperature are some of the physiological activities that have been controlled. It is not necessary, however, to purchase sophisticated equipment to control physiological processes. Learning how to relax or how to raise your level of activation can accomplish the same dramatic changes in autonomic functioning. Later chapters provide instructions to help you learn some of these skills.

There are two divisions of the autonomic nervous system that are important in understanding stress. The sympathetic division mobilizes the body to expend energy, preparing us for flight or fight by increasing the activity of the pituitary and adrenal glands. The parasympathetic branch generally functions to conserve energy during rest or relaxation.

LEARNING AND THE AUTONOMIC NERVOUS SYSTEM

Almost every response of the organ systems listed in chapter 1 can be elicited by a stimulus that was once neutral, that is, which would not ordinarily evoke that response. This type of learning is called "classical conditioning." Pavlov's conditioning experiments are well known. He sounded a buzzer as he gave food to a dog. The dog's natural and unlearned response to food was salivation. Prior to the experiment the bell did not produce salivation. After being paired with the food, the bell alone elicited salivation. (Incidentally, I have noticed that this same bell-salivation response holds for students who are in my noontime classes. When the bell rings they begin salivating in anticipation of lunch.) Vasodilation, vasoconstriction, contractions of the intestines, stomach contractions, and heart rate have been classically conditioned. This is a simple type of learning, but very important. Our emotional and stress responses are strongly dependent upon the autonomic nervous system. Our fears, for example, are learned. If we have an unpleasant experience with a stimulus or hold an unpleasant belief about that stimulus, it can bring about a series of autonomic reactions. A stimulus is any person, place, thing, or event in the environment or represented in the mind by images or ideas. The great variety of human experience accounts for the broad spectrum of human fears. Some people begin to have a "gut" feeling when another walks into the room. The feeling may be positive or negative. An important thing to remember is that because stress responses to stimuli are learned, they may be "unlearned." More specifically, a stimulus that elicits a sympathetic or stress response can through relearning come to elicit a relaxation or parasympathetic response. This is one of the principles involved in helping people overcome irrational fears or phobias. Such learning therapy techniques were developed in the 1930s.

Operant conditioning provides another model to understand how autonomic responses are learned. The probability that a given behavior will occur is dependent upon the stimuli that follow it. I have been fascinated by observing slot-machine players in Las Vegas. Some hold their breath, stand on one foot, hold the coin in very special ways, and pull the handle with all of the superstitious rituals that could fall within the realm of imagination. Those behaviors are repeated because they were being emitted at the time of a payoff. Some stimuli increase the probability of a response; others decrease the probability that a response will occur. Heart-rate acceleration, for example, has been shown to occur under operant control.

The entire general stress response, then, may come under stimulus control and accounts for part of the reason why one stressor causes tension stress in one person, but not in another.

Specific organ responses such as the pituitary-adrenal system are known to become conditioned to specific stimuli. A certain stimulus, for example, might cause certain blood vessels to contract causing a headache or stomach acid to be secreted in abundance in one situation and not in others. Some psychosomatic disorders such as stomach lesions or ulcers might be situationally caused.

THE PHYSIOLOGICAL-STRESS RESPONSE

The physiological-stress response can be initiated in two major ways. One way is to subject the body to extreme conditions such as heat, cold, injury, or disease. The second is dependent upon learning. These two pathways may lead to nearly identical responses: either a general stress response or a specific organ-system response. Figure 2 shows some of the steps in the psychophysiological stress response.

One important feature in this diagram is the double arrows between the event and perception. These show that our perception or interpretation of an event actually changes the nature and meaning of the event. This is a point of view contrary to traditional behavioristic psychology where the relationship is described as stimulus (S)–response (R)—a one-way relationship. A roller-coaster ride is a stressor, but might well be perceived as an exhilarating experience by one person, who buys another ticket, and as an unpleasant brush with eternity by another person, who would not ride again even for free.

UNCONSCIOUS PERCEPTION

Perception of an event is usually thought of as conscious, but sometimes there are unconscious elements in our perceptions. A good example can be seen in the building of frustration, anger, or tension that may accumulate throughout the day or week. Stimuli that escape your notice, but might be associated with past experiences, can increase tension and anxiety. If you try to think of specific events that have occurred to account for your increased tension stress, you may not come up with anything. Those little things do count, even the little things that escape your conscious awareness.

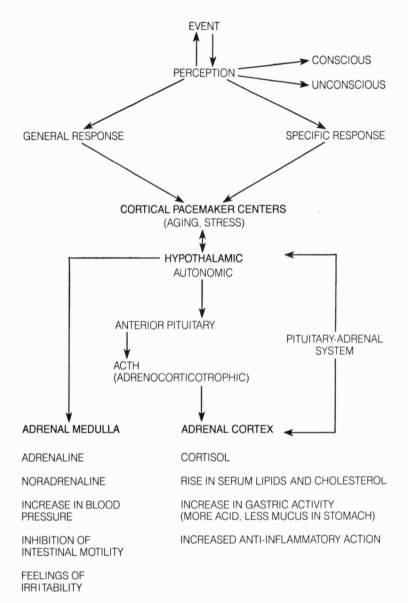

FIGURE 2 THE PSYCHOPHYSIOLOGICAL STRESS
RESPONSE

GENERAL ADAPTATION SYNDROME

The stress response of the body has been described by Hans Selye as the general adaptation syndrome (G.A.S.). The G.A.S. has three phases: an alarm reaction, a stage of resistance, and a stage of exhaustion. The temporal impact of the effects of prolonged stress becomes clear through Selye's model. In the alarm reaction a stressor causes a mobilization of the body's resources by activating the sympathetic division of the autonomic nervous system. This is also known as the emergency reaction. This emergency reaction leads to the initiation of adaptive or coping behaviors and the experience of pleasant or unpleasant emotions. Within a few minutes or hours, in most cases, we return to our own relative level of normal functioning. If the stressor persists, however, a second phase, the resistance phase, begins. Some of the emotional intensity of the alarm stage is reduced, the autonomic emergency reaction diminishes, stress hormone concentration decreases, and we cope with the situation. We have successfully adapted to the presence of a stressor. But this adaptation is costly because the body is consuming its energy supplies and the groundwork is being laid for the final phase of exhaustion. Exhaustion is most dramatically observed in animal research. Animals subjected to extreme and long-lasting stressful physical conditions show a marked deterioration of certain body organs. Death is also a possible consequence. In humans, chronic tension stress seems to be related to disease, but the relationship is not clear.

THE NERVOUS SYSTEM, AROUSAL, AND STRESS

The construct of arousal is central to understanding the relationship between nervous system activity and behavior. Adaptive stress and tension stress are dependent upon physiological arousal. It is useful to think of the total range of all human behavior on a continuum ranging from low arousal, for example, sleep (although some phases of sleep involve high arousal levels), to high arousal, which is characterized by the type of hyperexcitement seen in severe emotional disturbances. Indirect measures of arousal level are obtained from our physiological, psychological, and behavioral responses. Brain wave activity, autonomic nervous system activity such as heart rate, pituitary-adrenal activity, and behavioral performance can be used to measure arousal. Arousal level is increased from within by means of our thoughts, intentions, and images or from outside by stimuli that place demands upon our nervous systems. Arousal is correlated with stress. If a novel stimulus occurs in our environment, our nervous system increases its activity. We attend to the disturbance (orienting response) and assess its importance to us. If it is perceived as nonthreatening, our arousal level remains elevated for a short time, but we go on about our business. If the stimulus is repeated, our response patterns to it diminish. This is called *habituation*. A friend of mine resented her husband's apparent classification of her as a "habituated stimulus." When he came home in the evening, he read his paper and ignored her attempts at conversation. One evening, she wore a pair of fake glasses with a large false nose and moustache to capture his attention. He put down his paper, pretended that nothing was different, asked her what was being served for dinner, and continued reading without changing his expression. She understood the principle. He understood her message, but turned the joke around. If a stimulus is perceived as threatening or unpleasant, arousal level escalates into a defensive reaction. If we lose the ability to maintain the integration of our behavior and become disorganized in coping with a stressor, we have moved into the area of tension stress.

A major neural system mediating arousal is the reticular formation. It is a netlike system of neurons found in the brain stem between the major sensory fibers going to the brain and the motor fibers going from the brain to the muscles of the body. If you are drowsy and inactive and the telephone rings, the sensory impulses from the ringing stimulate the reticular formation, which in turn activates higher brain centers. Within a short time, you are able to function more effectively, although you may forget some of the earlier parts of the conversation. If the call brings you disastrous news, you might become overaroused. This would produce heightened emotions and disorganized behavior—tension stress.

The reticular formation is energized by increases in the number of sensory impulses bombarding the brain stem. Arousal can also be raised by increasing muscle tension. Noise, confusion, and increased muscle activity all increase arousal. Increases might be gradual or escape our notice until we begin to feel muscle tension or have a tension headache.

Muscles are composed of muscle fibers and specialized sensory-motor units called *spindle cells*. Spindle cells lie next to muscle fibers and signal the brain that the muscle is contracting. A unique feature of the spindle cell is that it also contains contractile fibers that may be activated by the brain or spinal cord. When they are, they cause the muscle fibers around them to begin to contract. Thinking about moving a certain muscle group causes the muscle spindles to send messages to the spinal cord and brain. This increases the muscle tone of the muscle that is to be involved in the contraction. Thinking of moving and actual physical movement raise arousal level. One of my seminar participants, upon hearing this, said that from then on he would exercise by thinking of moving rather than exerting himself with all of that physical movement. Unfortunately, that is not enough. Athletes warm up by exercising prior to a competition. Physical movement raises arousal level to one that is optimal for performance—to the stress window.

What keeps intense stimulation from automatically raising arousal to a level that is tension stress? Interpretation of the situation and labeling control the responses of our nervous system. We keep arousal within an adaptive range by perceiving that we control the situation. Only the most extreme physical conditions can force us into tension stress, and even then we know that it is possible for the mind to reign over physiology. In times of emergency, people have been known to suffer intense physical pain and maintain rational and purposeful behavior. The question is not *if* we can master our stress response to use it effectively, but *how* to use it.

HEREDITY AND STRESS

Hereditary predisposition to stress is important. This has been demonstrated in the cases of cardiovascular disease as well as schizophrenia. There is no sure way to determine whether we have a hereditary predisposition to develop a stress-related disorder. Clues may be cautiously found by examining the diseases of our blood relatives. If, for example, coronary disease runs in your family, it is possible that you might have some kind of genetic factor that will contribute to acquiring coronary disease, provided that you encounter certain environmental conditions. We cannot prove that, however. Furthermore, it is possible to modify lifestyle to achieve better health. Physical exercise, proper diet, learning how to relax, and learning how to use stress as an energy resource can be used to overcome part of the hand that heredity may have dealt us.

DIET, STRESS, AND NEUROTRANSMITTERS

At least two neurotransmitters vital to the stress response, serotonin and acetylcholine, cannot be directly manufactured by neurons. The precursors (building blocks) for these transmitters are obtained from the blood. Tryptophan, an amino acid, is taken from the blood to synthesize serotonin. Choline is taken to form acetylcholine. With every meal, the levels of these precursors rise and increase the rates at which neurons are able to produce and release their neurotransmitters into their synapses. When we are active, we consume greater amounts of these transmitters. If they are not available, our performance and mood suffer.

Serotonin is known to be an important transmitter in the limbic system, which is important for learning and emotional control, and the reticular formation, which regulates arousal. Deficits or excesses of these substances can cause severe mental and physical problems. Protein is important in the regulation of tryptophan. Although protein is a precursor, large amounts depress tryptophan levels and therefore result in a decrease of serotonin. Acetylcholine is one of the transmitters used in the brain, but it also enables our nerves to control our muscles. Myasthenia gravis is a disease related to a deficit of acetylcholine and results in muscular weakness and sometimes death. Choline is acetylcholine's precursor and is derived from lecithin-enriched foods such as eggs, soybeans, and liver.

One of the consequences of tampering with neurotransmitter systems is the disorder tardive dyskinesia. Tardive dyskinesia is a side effect that occurs from prolonged usage of antipsychotic drugs. The patient suffers from uncontrolled movements of the face, mouth, and tongue. These unpleasant symptoms persist long after the drug has been discontinued. It is hypothesized that tardive dyskinesia is due to a drug-induced deficit of acetylcholine in the brain. Dr. Richard Wurtman, professor of endocrineology and metabolism at M.I.T., has used choline with some success in treating patients with this disorder.

The ultimate dependency of brain functioning upon each meal is a further argument for a balanced diet. Fad diets, such as high-protein diets, should be avoided. Also remember that neurotransmitters exist in very small quantities, which are critically balanced. Caffeine, alcohol, nicotine, tranquilizers, barbiturates, and stimulants such as amphetamines all affect the relative concentrations of vital neurotransmitters. Hypoactivity, hyperactivity, and depression are possible outcomes of neurotransmitter imbalance.

DRUGS, THE NERVOUS SYSTEM, AND STRESS

The following table shows the major classes, therapeutic effects, and common side effects of drugs commonly used to treat tension-stress disorders. They are also used as muscle relaxants, antiemetics, and antimotion-sickness drugs. Drugs affect the nervous system by inhibiting or increasing the production of neurotransmitters, blocking the uptake of transmitters, increasing or decreasing the concentrations of body chemicals that enhance or suppress the production of transmitters, or affecting the excitability of the neuron itself. The phenothiazines, a group of major tranquilizers used as antipsychotic and muscle-relaxant drugs, for example, block the uptake of the neurotransmitters serotonin and dopamine.

Sedatives, hypnotics, minor tranquilizers, and major tranquilizers all depress the central nervous system to some degree. Alcohol is also a depressant. When it is taken along with any of the central nervous system depressants, it may produce a greater depression effect than would normally be expected. Many "accidental" suicides have been caused from drinking alcohol while taking central nervous system depressants.

All drugs have side effects. Side effects are unwanted consequences of medication that occur within the therapeutic dosage of a drug. The risk and discomfort of side effects must be weighed against a drug's therapeutic results. If you are taking a "minor" tranquilizer, do not be misled by the word *minor*. All antianxiety drugs have side effects. One

MAJOR CLASSES, THERAPEUTIC EFFECTS, AND
COMMON SIDE EFFECTS OF ANTIANXIETY DRUGS

DRUG	THERAPEUTIC EFFECTS	SIDE EFFECTS
DEPRESSANTS		
Barbiturates Amobarbital Butabarbital* Phenobarbital* Secobarbital	Depress the central nervous system; facilitate sleep	Habituation; tolerance; addiction; withdrawal; depress REM sleep; impair mental alertness, coordination; suicide danger
Nonbarbiturates Chloral hydrate Ethinamate Flurazepam Methaqualone Methyprylon		
NARCOTICS Morphine Codeine Meperidine Methadone	Relieve pain; depress central nervous system	Respiratory depression; habituation; tolerance; addiction; withdrawal
TRANQUILIZERS **Minor Tranquilizers** Benzodiazepines Clorazepate Chlordiazepoxide Diazepam Oxazepam	Relieve anxiety, tension; relax muscles	Drowsiness; lethargy; ataxia; headaches; hypotension; increase effects of alcohol; habituation; increasea tolerance; withdrawal
Other Antianxiety Drugs Chlormezanone Hydroxyzine Meprobamate		

MAJOR TRANQUILIZERS
(ANTIPSYCHOTIC DRUGS)

Phenothiazines Chlorpromazine Promazine Thioridazine Fluphenozine Trifluoperazine	Treat schizophrenia; quiet emotions; prevent nausea; relax muscles	Drowsiness; sedation; hypotension; tardive dyskinesia; lethargy; cardiac arrhythmias; skin pigmentation; liver impairment; photosensitivity
Butyrophenones **Thioxanthenes** **Rauwolfia Alka-** **loids**	Treat schizophrenia; quiet emotions	Mental depression; suicide potential; nightmares; insomnia; mental confusion; Parkinsonism; convulsions; diarrhea; increased gastric secretions, ulcers

*Commonly used to reduce anxiety

side effect that is rarely mentioned, however, is the impact of the drug on motivation. Many tranquilizers in addition to affecting the emotional areas of the brain also affect those areas that help energize us to achieve, to seek out goals, and to feel the effects of reward.

ALCOHOL, CAFFEINE, AND NICOTINE

Alcohol, caffeine, and nicotine are drugs that affect the nervous system. I am not going to tell you that you should not drink beverages containing alcohol and caffeine or that you should not smoke. But you should know that these drugs affect behavior by acting on the neuron, synapse, or the nerve-muscle junction. They are powerful.

Alcohol is a general depressant. It is not a stimulant. It

is mistaken for a stimulant because of the energetic behavior and euphoria that occur after a few drinks. These effects, however, can be attributed to alcohol's tranquilizing nature. If you drink enough of it, it becomes a sedative; and if you drink even more, an anesthetic. Although its effects upon the nervous system are complex, alcohol retards the uptake of neurotransmitters at their binding sites.

While I am writing this sentence, I am having some trimethylated xanthine (1, 3, 7-trimethylxanthine), which is the caffeine in my coffee. Caffeine is a stimulant and increases the production of neurotransmitters. Caffeinism is a recognized syndrome, a group of symptoms easily mistaken for a severe tension-stress reaction. The case of Cathy is an example.

Cathy complained of anxiety, loss of energy, depression, and shallow and rapid breathing. She was having difficulty sleeping. Her physician diagnosed her problems as being stress induced and prescribed Valium to reduce her tension. She took the Valium, but her problems persisted. She suffered a further loss of energy and found it difficult to function well in the afternoon. She also began to worry about using the drug as a crutch and tried to regulate her own medication. She wondered whether she could get through the day without taking a tranquilizer, and began counting her pills, worrying whether she would have enough to last through the week. She was a conscientious and competent manager of her family's home, but her energy was gone. The physician ruled out physical diseases and referred her to me for a psychological evaluation and possible psychotherapy. One item caught my attention during the initial interview. Cathy started her day with a cup of coffee, just as I do. But she followed that with a second, third, and so on. By the end of the day she had consumed between ten and fifteen cups of coffee. The evening dinner was an occasion for another two or three cups. She had been consuming 1,200 to 1,800 milligrams of caffeine each day. She was suffering from caffeinism. Caffeine is a powerful stimulant that produces symptoms similar to excessive tension. I asked her to reduce her coffee intake to two cups per day. At first she complained of a generalized throbbing headache and irritability. These are common symptoms of withdrawal from caffeine. After eight days she began to feel better. Her energy returned.

Caffeine dosages that exceed 250 milligrams (mg) daily are considered large. That is two cups of coffee. According to an article published in the April 1978 issue of *The Sciences* by Dr. John Grenden, 20 to 30 percent of adult Americans have a daily caffeine intake of over 500 to 600 milligrams. Disturbances in mood, sleep problems, and withdrawal symptoms are possible consequences of excessive caffeine consumption. One man told me that he had given up coffee without any difficulty. I asked him to share his method with the rest of the group He said, "It was simple. I drink Coke instead." He drank about five to eight cans of cola a day. He was consuming between 250 to 400 milligrams of caffeine in his daily cola intake. He promised to switch to decaffeinated coffee.

Nicotine affects the nervous system by increasing the effectiveness of a neurotransmitter secreted at the neuromuscular junction. The neuron secretes acetylcholine, which in turn initiates the muscle contraction. Nicotine effectively mimics acetylcholine in the nervous system and therefore has a stimulating effect.

I have included this brief discussion of alcohol, caffeine, and nicotine because they are drugs that are commonly used in high-stress situations. While we work, many of us drink coffee or cola and smoke cigarettes, cigars, or pipes. When the day is over, a little alcohol is used to take off the "edge." Many of us forget that these are powerful substances that affect the ability of our nervous system to produce stress energy. Excessive tension or lack of energy might, in part, be due to our intake of such drugs.

STRESS AND AGING

The Brain Endocrine Theory of aging states that neurons in higher brain centers act as pacemakers that regulate growth, aging, and death. These cells stimulate or inhibit special cells in the hypothalamus, a structure in the limbic system or emotional brain, which regulates endocrine secretions that control the major organ systems of the body. Stress causes changes in the types and rates of endocrine hormone secretions, which in turn influence the rate of aging. Research will have to show us the nature of the relationship between stress and the aging process as well as the means to control it. We know that in the normal process of aging, accelerated neuron death does not occur as we once thought it did. Nerve cells, however, do show a loss of dendrites and synaptic connections under certain conditions. There is good evidence to believe that these conditions are related to inactivity and a lack of stimulation.

HORMONES AND STRESS

Adrenocorticotrophic hormone (ACTH) is secreted by the anterior pituitary gland and is called the *stress hormone.* ACTH controls the activity of the adrenal cortex, which secretes over forty hormones, collectively known as adrenocortical steroids. These two glands together form the pituitary-adrenal system. Loss of these hormones can result in a drop in blood pressure and body temperature, muscular weakness, loss of appetite, kidney failure, and disturbances in the gastrointestinal tract. Hypofunction of the adrenal cortex is known as Addison's disease. The glucocorticoids are also secreted by the adrenal cortex. They are necessary for the maintenance of muscular strength, brain activity, and inhibition of inflammation. The secretions of the adrenal glands are powerful chemicals that support life itself. The energy for living is dependent upon this little pair of glands perched atop each of our kidneys. Even the ability to resist disease is strongly dependent upon the activity of the adrenals. It is no surprise to learn that they are called the *stress glands*.

Adrenaline and another hormone, noradrenaline, are secreted into the blood by the central portion of the adrenal gland, the adrenal medulla. The hypothalamus controls the adrenal medulla through neural connections. When adrenaline is secreted, the energy fuels of the body are released to prepare us to react.

STRESS AND RESISTANCE TO DISEASE

When a stressor places its demands upon the body, ACTH causes the adrenal cortex to secrete cortisol. Cortisol immediately causes a release of antibodies that are stored in the lymph nodes to protect the body from infection or disease. If stress is prolonged, there is an overall decrease in antibody production, which increases the body's susceptibility to bacterial and viral infection. Although there is little evidence to support the notion that stress might be related to cancer, if it is, the immunoresponse system of the body is the most likely link.

Excessive corticoid secretion can lead to stomach ulcers. The action of this body hormone is strong enough to produce ulcers within twenty-four to forty-eight hours. This happens because the production of stomach acid increases as the protective mucous lining of the stomach is reduced. Highly emotional states are not necessary—environmental demands alone can elicit the tension-stress response leading to stomach lesions or ulcers.

The biology of the immunity system is too complex to be described here, but two general types of immunologic problems that cause a great deal of human misery are autoimmune and hypersensitivity disorders. An autoimmune disease occurs when a normal body chemical changes and stimulates the body's antibody production. The body chemical then becomes treated as an antigen or foreign substance. It reacts against itself. Hypersensitivity disorders are exaggerated reactions to a foreign substance after prior exposure. These reactions are often painful and sometimes life-threatening. Hereditary predisposition is thought to play an important role in determining whether an individual will develop an immunologic disease. Excessive tension stress seems to trigger or aggravate many of these disorders. One of my students came to an examination wearing gloves. She told me that prior to each of my tests her hands would break out in a painful rash. She showed me her hands, and I was shocked to see the severity of her reaction. Worry over the impending examination seemed to precipitate her allergic reaction. After the examination was over, the irritation disappeared in a few days.

When the body fails to produce antibodies successfully and immunity fails, histamines may be released. Histamines produce many of the unpleasant consequences of the allergic reaction, such as hives, edema, and drippy nose. We know that the stress response affects the production of histamines as well as many of the hormones that are important for the immunoresponse. It is no surprise then that tension stress may aggravate or initiate an unpleasant immunologic disorder.

CAUSE AND EFFECT VERSUS CORRELATION

Everything seems to be a risk factor nowadays. Many if not most of the reports concerning risk factors for disease are based upon correlational studies.

A correlation is a statistical procedure that determines whether one variable or thing is related to another. A problem in the interpretation of correlations arises when it is mistakenly assumed that because two events are related, one event caused the other. A correlation between hat size and intelligence can occasionally be found within a classroom of students. If the correlation is a negative one, then the smaller the hat size, the greater the IQ score. If one believed that having a smaller head was indicative of greater intelligence, "head shrinking" would no longer be a metaphor for seeing an analyst, but a reality.

A cause-and-effect experiment is one in which an experimental condition is precisely controlled. The independent or experimental condition might be a drug, a virus, a certain level of stressor, or any condition that might produce an effect. That which is changed or influenced by the independent variable is called a dependent variable. Under the proper conditions of control, the relationships among independent variables and dependent variables are quantified, and a probability statement is made. Generally if we can say that the changes in the dependent variable could only have been produced by chance or measurement error five times or less out of one hundred, then we accept the relationship between the two variables as being one of cause and effect. The experiment must be replicated to be sure that the finding is reliable.

There are obvious problems in using the experimental method to study human physiology or behavior. We just cannot ethically administer drugs or stimuli that are potentially harmful to human beings. Studies involving human subjects must often rely upon correlational methods. If strong correlations between two variables are found over a long period of time, and if they are supported by experimental animal data, then we must take the correlation seriously and see what we can do to protect ourselves from a potential risk. Many risk-factor studies concerning the impact of stress on health are correlational. Not enough evidence is in to make statements about cause and effect.

STRESS AND CORONARY DISEASE

Common examples of correlational studies are found in coronary heart disease risk-factor research. Cardiovascular diseases such as high blood pressure have been studied extensively by correlating their incidence with blood cholesterol levels, cigarette smoking, and overweight. Some of the risk factors associated with coronary disease are listed below.

Physical Factors

Aging*

Sex (male)*

Elevated serum* cholesterol (250–275 mg per 100 ml or greater)

Elevated serum lipoproteins and triglycerides

Hypertension (blood pressure above 160/95 mm mercury)*

Dietary intake of animal fats and cholesterol

Heavy cigarette smoking (more than 20 per day)*

Diabetes mellitus*

Genetic factors

Other specific diseases (hypothyroidism)

Obesity

Psychological Factors

Psychological stress

Type A coronary-prone behavior pattern

Personality variables (possible risk factors, but they are not well substantiated)

Coping patterns

Physical inactivity

Left ventricle
hypertrophy*

---

*Listed by the American Heart Association, adapted from David C. Glass, **Behavior Patterns, Stress, and Coronary Disease,** New York: John Wiley & Sons, 1977.

Although relationships between these risk factors and cardiovascular disease have been found, there seems to be little direct evidence showing that reducing blood cholesterol or stress prevents cardiovascular disease. There is plenty of indirect evidence, however, that is motivating many of us to reduce our intake of animal fats. The risk factor is more clearly established for cigarette smoking. Similarly, if we examine the effectiveness of relaxation techniques upon the incidence of suspected stress-related diseases, we find at best the experimental evidence is weak. This does not mean that the many different relaxation and fitness techniques are not valuable. If they make us feel better, that would be enough.

We in the United States are becoming overly sensitized to the negative aspects of tension stress and we are overreacting. This has contributed to a misinterpretation of natural physiological and psychological stress responses. Many people believe that tension stress should not ever be a part of life. Millions are turning to professionals in medicine and mental health to help alleviate their feelings of tension and anxiety. Dr. David Mechanic, the director of the Center for Medical Sociology at the University of Wisconsin at Madison, studied the effects of psychological distress on an individual's perception of his/her own health and the use of medical and psychiatric facilities. He found that tension stress increases negative health perceptions and is comparable to the impact of serious, chronic illness in the use of medical services. His studies identify tension-stress distress as the single most important predictor of the use of medical and mental health services.

Occasionally, I meet with physicians who work in the medical services of large corporations. I am always compelled to ask two questions. One is, "How many of the people seen in the company's health clinic have disorders that seem to be due to excessive stress?" Most tell me that the majority of walk-ins suffer from tension-stress disorders. One physician asked me to estimate the number of clinic calls made for one year. I guessed 1,000, but the real number was over 7,000. In her *New York Times* article on stress, Kathy Slabogin reported that one New York company's health clinic saw an average of 2,400 employees per month. The second question that I ask is, "Do you think that tension stress causes disease?" Most answer by saying that it has not yet been proved that excessive stress causes disease. Some have answered no.

The fear of stress might motivate us to take better care of ourselves, but more often we are motivated to find quick cures for what are really natural and most often healthy physical and psychological reactions. This probably does more damage than the stress reaction itself. The reality of the matter is that stress is good for us, but we must learn more about it, and then learn to use it to our advantage

ENDORPHINS: MIND OVER BODY

Recently, specific opiate receptors have been found in the nervous system. This is an exciting prospect for researchers interested in the physiological basis of opiate addiction. The body produces its own opiatelike substances, enkephalen and endorphin. (These are two different substances with similar effects. I will use the term *endorphin* to refer to both.) They are a close match to synthetically produced opiates. It is hypothesized that excessive use of drugs such as heroin might suppress the body's production of its own opiates. When the supply of heroin is cut off a withdrawal syndrome occurs in response to the endorphin deficiency. It is possible that some of us have a genetic predisposition causing insufficient endorphin production, making us likely candidates for opiate addiction. Endorphins are important in regulating pain transmission in the nervous system. When Naloxone, a drug that blocks the body's endorphin receptors, is given during acupuncture treatment, the analgesic effects of acupuncture are diminished. Part of the pain-relieving effect of acupuncture seems to involve the release of endorphins by the stress of inserting the needles.

A finding that is important to our understanding of how our mind influences our body is seen in the placebo effect. Subjects who believe that they have received a pain-killer after surgery and actually have received a placebo report significant decreases in pain. If Naloxone is administered, perceptions of discomfort rise. Naloxone blocks the endorphins released by the body though subjects think they are receiving a pain-killer. When we expect relief, our body provides relief. Often after thoroughly examining patients who complain of typical tension-stress symptoms and ruling out physical disease, physicians will prescribe inert or placebo substances—the well-known "sugar pill." Patients frequently report great improvements. They believe that they are receiving medication and feel better. Some of the relief from unpleasant symptoms is probably due to the release of the body's endorphins or other neurotransmitters not yet discovered. In animals and humans, severe stress causes a rise in the body's available supply of endorphins. This helps reduce the pain that often accompanies stressful situations. Endorphins might also be involved in the causation of some types of schizophrenia. Double-blind studies are now being conducted to test this hypothesis. A double-bind study is one in which both the experimenter and the subject do not know who is receiving the active drug and who is receiving the placebo. Double-blind studies must be conducted precisely because of the tendency of human beings to feel better when they think there is a reason to feel better. Endorphin research is a convincing argument for the power of mind over body as well as the positive nature of the stress response.

SELF-CONTROL, THE BODY, AND STRESS

The stress response is made possible by delicate body chemistry. Stress hormones cause increased production of neurotransmitters. They in turn enable the nervous system to be aroused to higher levels of functioning. Brain stem structures such as the reticular activating system move the emotional and decision-making areas of the rest of the brain into a state of preparedness. Information is processed more efficiently. The senses are alerted to detect stimuli that are psychologically important to us. The stress response will be maintained as long as it is necessary to meet the demands placed upon us. It will also persist as long as we believe preparedness is necessary. Our fears are learned. We are not born with them. Throughout our life, many situations, objects, and people become associated with various levels of arousal. We label our experience as favorable or unfavorable. These stimuli come to elicit arousal levels and feeling states when they are present in our thoughts or actually confront us in our physical environment. Because we do learn to perceive stimuli as stressors, we can "unlearn" them. New responses, more adaptive ones, may be learned to replace older maladaptive ones. This is the hope and promise of learning and practicing self-control.

If we perceive that we are no longer in control of life events, our arousal level can reach the tension-stress level. Tension stress leads to behavioral and mental disorganization. We become less able to cope, which leads to more tension. Neurotransmitters and stress hormones become unbalanced. If we turn to drugs, we find that our problems are not solved; and even worse, we find that unwanted side effects cause us more problems. Drugs often suppress our motivation and energy to get things done.

On the other hand, if we can learn to harness stress—keep it within constructive bounds—we can expect to collect its benefits. Enhanced behavioral performance, increased resistance to disease, increased mental capacity, and vital feelings of well-being are positive contributions of adaptive stress. Our nervous system produces its own chemicals, such as the endorphins, to ease our passage through the inescapable difficulties of life.

3: MIND OVER STRESS

What you think and *how* you think are more important in determining your stress reaction than most of the physical stressors from the environment. The basic structures and physiological processes discussed in chapter 2 are critical to the stress response, but rarely do they, on their own, trigger tension and anxiety. In most cases of depression, for example, it is not appropriate to say that a person is depressed because his or her neurotransmitters have been depleted. If that should happen, however, psychological depression is a possibility. What we must really do is to try to understand how mental functioning might bring about a depletion of neurotransmitters, and how and why we assign labels such as "depression" or "unpleasant" to our experience. Using your stress energy to feel better is not simply a matter of convincing yourself that everything will turn up roses if you think positively. That helps in some situations, but hurts in others, particularly if things get worse.

PERCEIVED CONTROL

We must learn how the mind controls the stress response and then learn and practice skills that will give us greater control. We need to have the experience of being in control to be able to experiment with using stress energy as a resource to accomplish our goals and to feel better. Perceived control is a psychological concept extensively studied by psychologists David Glass of the City University of New York and Jerome E. Singer of the Uniformed Services University of Health Science, Bethesda, Maryland. It is the perception of being able to do something; of *not* feeling helpless; and akin to feeling that we can achieve. Before you read further, try assessing your own perceived control of the important stressors and stress reactions operating in your life.

SCALING

The lists of common stress indicators and possible psychosomatic disorders and the tension-stress test in chapter 1, and the sources of stress and stress reactions listed in chapter 5, will help you complete this task. The control scale on the next page and the following steps will enable you to measure your own levels of control.

First, list in order, from the most important to the least, the stressors (events, persons, places, or objects) that are important to you in daily life. Then list in order, from the most important to the least, as many of your psychological and physical stress reactions as you can. Use the scale of perceived control to measure each stressor and stress reaction that you listed by rating each on a seven-point scale. A score of 1 means that the stressor or stress reaction is *not under your control.* You feel that you cannot do much about it. A score of 7 means that it is *completely under your control.* For example, if you experience feelings of tension, anxiety, or panic and they are not under your control, you might assign a value of 1 or 2.

SCALING PERCEIVED CONTROL

EVENT, PERSON, PLACE, OBJECT	NOT UNDER MY CONTROL AT ALL					COMPLETELY UNDER MY CONTROL
_____	1 2 3 4 5 6 7					
_____	1 2 3 4 5 6 7					
_____	1 2 3 4 5 6 7					
_____	1 2 3 4 5 6 7					
_____	1 2 3 4 5 6 7					
_____	1 2 3 4 5 6 7					

PSYCHOLOGICAL
AND PHYSIOLOGICAL
STRESS REACTIONS

_____	1 2 3 4 5 6 7
_____	1 2 3 4 5 6 7
_____	1 2 3 4 5 6 7
_____	1 2 3 4 5 6 7
_____	1 2 3 4 5 6 7

Total the circled numbers
and divide by the number of
items rated for both stressors
and stress reactions to obtain
average control score.

$$\frac{\text{Stressors total}}{\text{number of items}} = \underline{\quad\quad} = $$

$$\frac{\text{Stress reactions}}{\text{number of items}} = \underline{\quad\quad} = $$

When you have scaled all of the list, total the numbers circled for the stressors and divide by the number of stressors to get an average control score. Then do the same for the stress responses. The average score will give you some idea of how you perceive your ability to control your own stress responses and stressors effectively.

If your perceived control scores for both stressors and stress reactions are 3 or below, then you might well be experiencing depression, anxiety, or both. If you have a high perceived control score for stressors, but a low one for stress reactions, then you are controlling events around you, but you are not in control of your own stress response and should learn how to relax.

HOW OUR THOUGHTS CONTROL STRESS

We all have heard stories about people healing themselves, keeping themselves alive, or accomplishing seemingly impossible physical or psychological tasks. I am always fascinated by these stories, but somehow I think to myself that they are not genuine because they are not scientifically verified. But there is a plausible explanation for some of these phenomena. Both adrenaline and noradrenaline, as you will recall from the last chapter, are secreted from the adrenal medulla in response to perceived stressors. One important effect of adrenaline secretion is to increase the arousal level of the nervous system and the rest of the body. Professor Marianne Frankenhaeuser, head of Experimental Psychology Research Unit, Swedish Medical Research Council, has shown that there are reliable relationships between the levels of arousal and performance, and adrenaline and noradrenaline levels. Increases and decreases of adrenal secretions may be measured through urinalysis. It is possible, therefore, to relate the secretion of the body's stress hormones to our emotions, problem-solving strategies, and performance. These data provide us with many exciting leads for using stress to our advantage. What you *think* influences

your stress arousal as effectively as any environmental demand. Furthermore, perceptions of mastery or control in
stressful situations decrease adrenal secretions. In one experiment (Frankenhaeuser and Rissler, 1970), three conditions, each reflecting a different situational control, were
administered to subjects. Urinalysis of each control condition showed that as the subject gained more control over a
stressor, an electric shock in this experiment, adrenaline
levels decreased.

Generally, pituitary-adrenal secretions parallel levels of
behavioral arousal. Pituitary-adrenal secretions, then, increase during excitement and decrease during states of
calm. These secretions regulate metabolism, growth, sexual
activity, and our ability to resist disease.

Undesirably or unacceptably low levels of activity and
stimulation, however, actually increase pituitary-adrenal
secretions. When activity and environmental stimulation
falls below our perceived level or what we think they
should be, we experience tedium and boredom. Clock
watching, fidgeting, pacing, and sighing are only some of
the behavioral signs of monotony and boredom. Having
that much adrenaline and that high an arousal level is like
"being all dressed up with no place to go." Herein lies a
clue to one of the most important functions critical to our
feeling of control—critical to using stress rather than having stress use us.

We estimate or mentally appraise the energy requirements of the potential stressors that we confront each day.
A stressor often evokes an automatic, learned stress response. We define various persons, places, events, and objects around us as being psychologically important. Hence
they, according to how we label them, raise or lower our
hormones and stress. When a stressor is perceived, we must
mobilize enough energy to deal with it. Even though some
stimuli escape our conscious awareness, they are influential.
That is how those little things can add up to elicit a larger-

than-needed stress response. Hyperstress produces performance decrements in situations where the number of cues or amount of information bombarding us is high and we are not able to sort out the information needed to do the job. If the number of cues is small and the task simple, performance may improve. If we do not mobilize enough energy to meet the demand, our psychological and physical performance suffers.

ACCEPTING THE INEVITABLE

Adaptive stress is partially dependent upon physical stressors. It is also dependent upon our ability to make accurate assessments of the amount of energy required to cope with any situation. Once we label a situation as being beyond our control and unpleasant, then our stress increases to unhealthy or inappropriate levels. If we *accept* a situation as being beyond our control, then our stress level might not become elevated. The word *accept* is the key. It means that you have thought of the realistic coping responses available and realize that you cannot change things. You should then control your stress response. Driving in heavy traffic can be a test of your ability to accept the thought that you have little control over a situation. If you are trapped in a long line of traffic and are late for an appointment, there is not much you can do to get free. You still have choices, however. You can swear, sweat, and stress-up. You can jump out of your car and start kicking fenders. Or you can use the time constructively to relax or to plan your day or week while listening to music on the car radio. It will do you little good to get "uptight." The excess stress energy should be used for activities that are beneficial.

STRESS CUES

Before any decisions are made on what to do in a stressful situation, try to become aware of the relevant or important stimuli. Any stimulus that is psychologically important to you is called a cue. Our ability to process information is dependent upon our stress level. When we are hyperactive, we can process too much information and tend to process the irrelevant rather than the relevant cues. In that case behavior seems to be inappropriate or ineffective. Panic is a likely outcome as demonstrated in the following example.

A systems engineer who worked for a power utility was monitoring a power grid display. Suddenly warning lights began flashing. He was trained to deal with such emergencies, but had not reviewed or rehearsed procedures for some time. His response during the emergency can only be described as panic. He said, "My mind was racing. I began running up and down the board. I was confused and began throwing switches without thinking." Retrospectively, he said that his anxiety had been gradually increasing for months. Although he had not realized that he was tense, his family had but did not wish to trouble him further by bringing it up. When the emergency struck, the additional demand threw him into panic. The almost countless irrelevant stimuli in the room flooded his awareness and he was not able to maintain the organization of his behavior. As soon as he began to experience panic, he said to himself, "I can't handle this—the whole damned thing is going to go down!" There is his labeling process. When he labeled the situation as overwhelming and himself as helpless, he gave up. Later he realized that at that point the day could still have been saved.

VICIOUS STRESS CYCLES

When stress increases to a level that captures our awareness, we become aware of increased heart rate, perspiration, and other physical signs of arousal. Sometimes awareness of intense stress breeds more stress and deceives us into believing that matters are worse than they really are. The misinterpretation of bodily responses and the confusion arising from ineffective cue sampling often lead to faulty labeling and panic. Cardiac panic is an example of this kind of problem. Fear of a heart attack increases heart rate, breathing, and anxiety. These reactions in turn are interpreted as evidence of a heart attack. Finally, the person experiencing all of this might even lose consciousness and, when regaining consciousness, might believe that he or she has had a genuine heart attack. Fortunately cardiac panic is rare. All episodes of apparent cardiac irregularity should be brought to the attention of a physician immediately. When perceptions of control diminish and we feel that we are not able to do anything that will help, we are helpless. Learned helplessness accounts for much of the frustration and depression in our society.

LEARNED HELPLESSNESS

Learned helplessness occurs when individuals learn to perceive that their responses have little or no effect upon the rewards and punishments that they receive. Voting behaviors and attitudes of a large segment of the American public are a good example. The expression, "Why vote? It doesn't make any difference anyway; nothing is going to change," reflects perceived helplessness.

Originally the concept of learned helplessness was investigated in the laboratory through carefully controlled studies using animals as subjects. Animals were placed in hostile environments where they were exposed to adverse situations. Barriers prevented them from escaping. Animals learned that reinforcement (in this case, shock or some other unpleasant stimulus) and responding were independent. In other words, it did not matter what an animal did; it still received the shock. Such learning reduces the initiation of positive-coping responses. If the barriers were removed so that the animal could easily run into another compartment and escape the shock, they would not. They would suffer the pain of the shock rather than attempt to escape even when the opportunity was available. Incidentally, it was often necessary to drag or shove the animal into the safe compartment a number of times before it would attempt to escape on its own.

EFFECTS OF LEARNED HELPLESSNESS

Chronic learned helplessness fosters a number of emotional, cognitive, motivational, and behavioral consequences. Emotional effects include fear, anxiety, depression, and even psychosomatic disorders. Cognitive effects include negative expectations with respect to trying new responses and feelings of helplessness, hopelessness, and powerlessness. Motivational effects include the reduction of the initiation of new responses, loss of interest, decreases in energy and ambition, and reduced interest in eating and sexual activities. The most severe problem emerging out of learned helplessness is depression.

Depression can occur at either end of a behavioral arousal continuum that ranges from inactivity to hyperactivity. One type, motor depression, is characterized by loss of energy and general slowing down of bodily processes. The pace of walking, speech, and even digestive processes is slowed. Agitated depression is characterized by anxiety and restlessness. Both types of depression are psychologically similar. Common psychological symptoms are sadness, crying spells, self-hatred, loss of sense of humor, nega-tive self-concept, and feelings of hopelessness. Some of the physical signs of depression are loss or abnormal increase in appetite, waking up during the night, loss of energy, restlessness, decrease in sexual interest and/or activity, con-stipation, diarrhea, and physical illness. The case of Barbara will illustrate a common depressive reaction.

Barbara, aged fifty-three, worked as a homemaker. Her children were raised and had families of their own. Her first husband had died, and she remarried. She got up early, cooked breakfast for her husband, did all of the housework, and prepared his meals when he came home. His attitude toward her was cold and uncaring. He did not seem to understand how hard she worked in their home. He only seemed to complain. They seldom went out or entertained; and if they did, he wanted to come home early. She began to feel tense and eventually became depressed. Tranquiliz-ers helped her sleep and relax, but her depression wors-ened. (Incidentally, tranquilizers are often discouraged in the treatment of depression because they are themselves central nervous system depressants.) She felt helpless, de-pressed, lonely, and trapped. She thought that she had done something wrong. After dinner in the evening, her husband would fall asleep in his chair, and if she watched TV or made any noise, he would wake up in a foul mood and tell her to be quiet because he needed his rest. She felt that she could not do anything short of divorce to better her situation. She began to lose weight. Her health was begin-ning to fail. Finally, her sister made a therapy appointment for her.

She discovered that because she had labeled her situa-tion as hopeless and herself as powerless, she had narrowed her perception of alternatives to improve her situation. Her therapy plan helped her divert stress energy into initiating new behaviors. She began to feel anger toward her hus-band. Anger can be useful in breaking out of helplessness, but it must be guided. Together, we developed specific behavioral objectives for each week. She informed her husband that she was going out on two afternoons to visit friends. She did that, enjoyed herself, and regained some of her self-confidence. The newly gained confidence helped her to develop new behavioral objectives. She became more assertive. Lest you think that this was all an unpleasant surprise for her husband, part of her behavioral objectives were devoted to communicating with him. She did not seek permission or approval, but explained her objections to him. During our last meeting she told me that she felt "great." She had joined a bowling team and had established a group of friends. Her husband's attitude toward her improved, and they began going out each week. Her tension-stress symptoms disappeared. Not only had she diverted some of her stress energy toward constructive behaviors, but she also created more energy by assigning specific behavioral objectives to be accomplished each week. Structuring life activity by setting goals focuses energy. It enables us to identify our successes clearly. We can see that our actions produce results, and begin to perceive that we are in control.

OVERCONTROL: A SURE ROAD TO DISASTER

Much has been written about Type A and Type B behaviors. Drs. Meyer Friedman and Ray Rosenman are pioneers in research relating behavior patterns to coronary disease. Unfortunately their work has been interpreted by some to mean that there are Type A and Type B personality types. There is not much support for personality types per se, but there is considerable evidence to support the notion that certain learned behavioral patterns contribute to chronic tension stress. Type A behavior is characterized by competitiveness, striving, exaggerated concern for time and deadlines, and aggressiveness. Type B behavior represents a somewhat opposite pattern. Cooperativeness, concern for others, and little concern for time pressures are common characteristics of Type B behaviors. We can, and often do, engage in both types of behaviors. They are at opposite ends of a single behavioral scale. Most of us show both Type A and Type B behaviors in our life. If either type of behavior is prolonged, however, we might begin to develop problems. Excessive striving, worry over deadlines, and aggressiveness over-drive the stress mechanisms of the body. On the other hand, chronic underactivity is not healthy either.

There is evidence suggesting that the greater amounts of noradrenaline secreted during increased stress cause small lesions in the walls of coronary arteries. These lesions heal, but the scars are thought to become sites for the ac-cumulation of cholesterol or other fatty deposits that could eventually clog arteries. All of these factors in addition to all of the other chronic physiological stress reactions are proba-bly related to coronary heart disease.

Perceiving that we are in control leads to a decrease in adrenaline and noradrenaline secretion by the adrenal glands. But overstriving to control produces increased stress hormone secretion. The "if you want something done right, do it yourself" philosophy is an example of an overcontrol syndrome. There are many things that we can control, some that can be partially controlled, and others over which control is not possible. Attempts to overcontrol will automatically fail in the long run. It is just not possible to control everything. Initially, overcontrol produces hyper-activity or overarousal. Eventually overarousal interferes with our cue-sampling ability. The results are mental confu-sion, disorganized behavior, and, as described in the case of the systems engineer, labeling the situation as hopeless and the self as helpless. Depression and inactivity are com-mon consequences. Then, the cycle begins all over again. Many of these behavioral patterns become fixed and are sometimes mistaken for personality types. They are resistant to change but can be changed by learning new ways to cope with stressors.

THE NEED FOR POWER AND STRESS

Dr. David McClelland has been studying the need for power (n power) for a number of years. He has developed an n power test. High scorers are described as aggressive, competitive, prestige-conscious, and argumentative. High n power scorers often have difficulty in sleeping, which, by the way, has been shown to be correlated with high adrenaline levels. The Type A behavior and high need for power patterns produce common problems stemming from high arousal levels. Conflicts between n power and intense desires to succeed can qualify us as candidates for the over-control syndrome or Type A behavior patterns.

SEX DIFFERENCES AND STRESS

Studies have shown that females do not show the increases in adrenaline that men do to the same stressors (Johansson and Post, 1974). One explanation of this lower adrenaline secretion is related to the traditional role expectations imposed on women in a traditionally male-oriented society. It is an unfortunate stereotype, but men have claimed the role of the aggressor, the competitor, the achiever, and the breadwinner. Men typically show the Type A behavior pattern more frequently than women. Men also have higher mortality rates for coronary heart disease than women. As women learn to become more competitive, their adrenaline production might increase to higher levels during stress. But let me emphasize that there is little current evidence to suggest that women will suffer increases in cardiovascular disease because of their fuller participation in the work force. This is discussed more fully in chapter 10, Stress and Work.

PERCEPTION AND STRESS

Perception is the reception and processing of information provided by the sense organs. The physiological processes of perception lie outside of consciousness, but the end results are the data that enable us to survive. Perception as a process involves the total person: physiology, ideas, emotions, and past experience as recorded in the memory. The continual flow of perceptual information is added to the context of past experience to orient us toward the future. Awareness and perception are related. The ability to process information is dependent upon arousal level. We know that we do not sense or subsequently process all of the information impinging upon us at any one time. Attention is selective. We attend to stimuli that are important to us. Occasionally someone will tell me that he reads and listens to music or watches TV at the same time, and therefore is able to attend to more than one thing at a time. What is really happening, however, is that attention is rapidly shifting back and forth between one event and the other. This has been called the "cocktail-party phenomenon." Imagine yourself at a party with a large number of people in the room. You are conversing with one person, but more interested in what someone else is saying. Chances are you will remember more of the conversation that interested you more, but still function fairly well in the less interesting conversation. But make no mistake, performance in your conversation will be impaired.

Certain stimuli become "tagged." This ensures that we will shift our attention to them when they occur. Some tags are acquired through conditioning and some are intentionally assigned. Attitudes, opinions, and beliefs form internal frames of reference or mental-sets. Mental-sets are relatively stable templates that help organize our sensory experiences into meaningful ideas, judgments, and emotions.

LABELING

Labeling is naming. Labeling can be self-serving, prejudiced, oversimplified, or ambiguous. Labeling is a behavior subject to all of the rules of learning. It is not dependent upon heredity and beyond our control. Some of our labels are reinforced; some are punished. Some of them cause fear; some joy. Many, if not most, elicit stress. Labels represent our mental-sets, which we communicate by speech or writing. Our ability to discriminate between harmless and dangerous stimuli can be hampered by faulty labeling. If that happens, too much energy is produced and the excess energy is often perceived as tension.

CONTROL-SETS AND GOOD STRESS

Control-sets are realistic ideas that help us make accurate energy assessments of the key stressors affecting us at any given time. They are highly individualized in expression because they are unique products of each person's experience. Two categories of maladaptive or tension-stress sets are no-control sets, which occur during learned helplessness, and overcontrol-sets, which are found in the Type A and high-need-for-power behavioral patterns. Control-sets, on the other hand, support the acquisition of adaptive behavior patterns that help produce adaptive-stress energy. Good feelings about oneself, often referred to as feelings of self-esteem, flow from the perceived ability to be effective— to be competent. We must perceive that what we do produces results or reinforcements that are consequences of our actions. There are two general groupings of skills that help us develop control sets. One group involves perceptual skills and the other behavioral structuring skills.

PERCEPTION AND JUDGMENT

How we perceive an event or stimulus is dependent upon the total context in which it occurs. Our behavior is then dependent upon that perception. Using series of various sensory stimuli, Professor Harry Helson, an experimental psychologist, showed that perceptual judgments of the intensity or quality of a specific stimulus are dependent upon the magnitudes of all other similar stimuli in a given series. A subjective midpoint, the adaptation level, emerges whenever we are making judgments. If, for example, you are trying to find a shade of green paint for your living room that is pleasant to your eye, you might look at all of the green paint chips or samples, side by side. They are often arranged on sample cards from the lightest to the darkest shades. Suppose that there are seven shades in the green series, each one separated by an equal interval of color (saturation). One shade will appear to be the middle shade of green. Everything below the midpoint is lighter and everything above darker. This midpoint, however, does not correspond to the actual physical midpoint of the series, that is, chip number 4. A subjective midpoint emerges and this is the adaptation level. It can be measured and quantified, and is useful in studying our responses to stressors. All of your judgments will be influenced by this value. Everything below that value will be judged as lighter and everything above as darker. But what is light for one series might be judged dark in another series that contains more light shades. This shift, however, takes time, and several exposures to the new series are necessary. Many hideously intense green living rooms have similar epitaphs: "I thought that this shade of green was light and fresh, until I put it on the wall and then it was terrible." This concept of adaptation level applies to judging the pleasantness and unpleasantness of stressors. It is involved in the determination of subjective statements as to how much we "can take"—our stress-tolerance level.

In one of the experiments conducted in our lab, subjects received two series of electric shocks. They received one shock at a time and had to judge whether that shock was weak or strong as compared to the other shocks in the series. Shock intensities in the series were arranged so that shocks judged as strong in series 1, because they fell above the adaptation level, would be judged as weak in series 2, because they fell below the adaptation level. Data for twenty subjects indicate that what is judged strong and unpleasant in one series is judged as weak and tolerable in another. Our perception of what is painful or unpleasant changes depending upon the severity of the situation. Furthermore, different individuals adapted more quickly (fast shifters) to the new series of stressful stimuli. We are now conducting research to determine how perceptions of control are related to the ability to adapt to new stressful stimuli. Preliminary data indicate that fast shifters who perceive that they have little internal control over life events seem to adapt to new stressors more quickly than slow shifters who perceive that they are in control. The fast shifters also have higher tension levels.

The formation of adaptation levels can cause errors in judgment. It is often necessary to "override" unpleasant labeling. The way to do this is to mentally remove a stressor from its context; don't look at it in terms of the unpleasantness of the past, but evaluate it in the context of the present. Look at the general picture. Expand your awareness to perceive as many cues as possible. During this process, labeling should be avoided or set aside. From this enriched field of perceived cues, select those that are the most significant guides for behavior. For example, if you are trying to work and you find that your tension level is increasing to a level that is interfering, identify the specific cues that contribute to this tension and develop a behavioral strategy to deal with them.

BEHAVIORAL STRUCTURING: HOW TO BE EFFECTIVE

Using the same example of the work situation, you might move to a quieter work area, shut a door, arrange your tasks into priorities, or do anything else that would produce results. The point is that you should learn to identify specifically behavioral courses of action that will lead to concrete results. This helps avoid learned-helplessness-sets by making the relationship between behavior and its consequences clear. Behavioral structuring is the process of identifying specific behavioral objectives, all of which ultimately lead to some greater goal.

Students occasionally come into my office discouraged and ready to give up their studies. They have identified a life goal, for example to become an engineer or physician. But when they begin their studies, they often have not identified the objectives necessary to achieve their goals. They jump in without identifying the relevant cues or structuring their behaviors. The result is that minor failures turn into helplessness-sets and giving up. One low grade in freshman chemistry discourages some able students from pursuing their career choices. The same kind of thing happens when some of us try dieting. Our objective is to lose weight; but how, how much, and when? The objectives are too general and do not lend themselves to producing tangible results. One piece of candy or cake, therefore, sparks the helplessness-set—"I can't do this." A college adviser can help a student structure his/her behaviors by setting specific objectives and selecting relevant cues. In the chemistry course example, the specific behaviors necessary to pass chemistry should be identified. Passing chemistry is one step toward the successful achievement of the career goal. Stress energy is diverted into powering adaptive behaviors. It might even be necessary to create more energy to improve performance.

Behavioral structuring can improve performance on complex tasks during increased stress. Of course, life is not a rosy succession of win-win situations. Sometimes we are going to fail, but even when we do, our perception of control can be enhanced, provided we are able to identify specific behaviors that need to be replaced or improved rather than saying, "I failed. I can't do anything right. There is no point in trying." Perceiving that you are in control holds the physiological stress response of the body within a healthy range and leads to feelings of exhilaration and increased self-esteem.

4: USING STRESS ENERGY TO OVERCOME DEPRESSION AND BOREDOM

Depression and boredom are common complaints of millions of people. Depression is said to be a problem in the life of one out of every five persons in the United States. We should expect to have occasional feelings of boredom and depression and not regard them as unnatural or indicative of serious problems. If either one is prolonged, however, then we should do something about it.

PHYSICAL AND PSYCHOLOGICAL SYMPTOMS OF DEPRESSION

Depression is a complex physical and psychological state sometimes marked by hypoactivity and at other times hyperactivity. A depressed person may greet you with a smile— a smile that masks feelings of dejection and helplessness. The second edition of the American Psychiatric Association's *Diagnostic and Statistical Manual of Mental Disorders* (1968) lists some eight types of depression, ranging from the depressive neuroses to the more severe psychotic depressions. Chronic depression can pose psychiatric and physical problems if not recognized and dealt with effectively. The Individual Depression Scale that follows will help identify some of the early signs of depression. The important symptoms of depression are listed in the left-hand column.

INDIVIDUAL DEPRESSION SCALE

Circle the number that indicates the appropriate frequency of the behaviors listed under symptoms of depression.

SYMPTOMS OF DEPRESSION	FREQUENTLY	ONCE IN A WHILE	RARELY
PHYSICAL			
Decrease in appetite	2	1	0
Waking up during night	2	1	0
Lack of energy	2	1	0
Constipation/diarrhea	2	1	0
Decline in sexual activity		YES (2)	NO (0)
EMOTIONAL			
Feelings of sadness	2	1	0
Crying	2	1	0
Self-anger	2	1	0
Loss of sense of humor		YES (2)	NO (0)
Flattening of emotions, i.e., decrease in feeling		YES (2)	NO (0)
MOTIVATIONAL			
Loss of interest in work	2	1	0
Loss of interest in leisure-time activities	2	1	0
Decrease in sexual interest	2	1	0
COGNITIVE			
Negative outlook	2	1	0
Self-blame	2	1	0
Feelings of helplessness or lack of control	2	1	0

TOTAL POINTS ———

SCORE
21–32 Depression probable
12–20 Depression possible
 0–11 Depression not probable

If your score falls between 20 and 30, it is recommended that you visit your physician for a physical examination. Depression often arises from physical illness and this should be checked before assuming that lifestyle factors are producing depression. The average score for four hundred subjects taking this scale is 13.6.

It should be no surprise to find that the psychiatric classification system for depression is rather complicated. Endogenous, exogenous, primary, secondary, unipolar, and bipolar are some of the types of depression.

Endogenous depression is a relatively severe disorder. Hereditary and biological factors seem to be important in its occurrence. Studies on twins indicate that if one of a pair of identical twins is raised apart from the other and develops a severe depression, the correlation is high for the other to do the same. Some types of depression, therefore, seem to have hereditary roots.

Exogenous depression is less severe and more dependent upon learning. It is a reaction to current stressors. Temporary loss of a job, failure, or the death of someone close are expected to produce depression. Major surgery or poor health, for example, frequently produce depression. Postoperative depression is related to the physical impact of surgery and the patient's expectations about the difficulty of recovery. Two of my clients who had ovarian cysts removed complained of excessive anxiety, depression, physical discomfort, and lack of energy. They did not know what to expect after surgery and felt that they were not recovering as quickly as they should. Both were advised by their physicians that another surgery might be necessary. Physicians making second opinions for both patients explained that their depression and physical discomfort were to be expected and that further surgery was not necessary. We need to pay more attention to the psychological impact of surgery and other medical procedures. Recovery is dependent upon psychological as well as physical factors.

Primary and secondary depression are distinguished from each other by the fact that secondary depression is superimposed upon another emotional disorder such as a neurosis or psychosis. Unipolar depression is characterized by feelings of depression alone. Bipolar includes swings in mood from depression to mania.

One of the important biological correlates of depression is a deficiency in certain neurotransmitters. Noradrenaline is a leading candidate for depression. There is some disagreement among scientists as to whether a deficiency of noradrenaline produces depression and learned helplessness or whether it is the other way around. There is good evidence to suggest that both cases are valid. The majority of everyday depressions are situationally precipitated and can be eliminated without the use of drugs.

COMBATING DEPRESSION

DRUGS

Mood-elevating drugs, the antidepressants, are prescribed by the millions to give relief from depression. They do so by increasing the quantity or effectiveness of the body's supply of neurotransmitters. Unfortunately, depressive symptoms usually are only temporarily suppressed by antidepressants. If the drug is withdrawn, depression often returns. Use of antidepressants alone does not particularly help a person to develop feelings of control or to learn new coping skills. Taking a drug for the relief of depression is another way of saying, "I am helpless," or, "Things are out of control."

The side effects of the most commonly used antidepressants, the tricyclics, can suppress the energy that is needed to break out of depression. Other common side effects are dizziness, weakness, lethargy, drowsiness, and headache. Some patients eventually show mania or hyperactivity when taking antidepressants and are given tranquilizers to calm down.

ANTIDEPRESSION STRATEGIES

An expenditure of energy is required to get rid of depression—energy that might be in short supply. The effort should involve the planning and execution of specific behaviors that will produce positive effects. In most cases of reactive or situational depressions, it is possible to raise arousal level through emotions such as anger and amusement, or novel sensory stimulation and physical activity, for example, exercise or sexual activity. Sometimes relief is only temporary. What is needed for more permanent success is to learn new adaptive coping behaviors to deal with the situation that is causing the depression. It is best not to think of the entire situation but rather to identify smaller things that can be done to get yourself going and also help solve the problem. Behavioral structuring, which is discussed in chapter 3, is helpful. As each small objective is achieved, not only are you another step closer to resolving the problem, but with each step you can perceive that your behaviors are producing results. The experience of success shatters negative mental-sets.

If you decide to try to solve the problem by getting out of the situation or trying to put it out of your mind, that is fine. That works sometimes. But most often it is not enough to take vacations from depressive situations unless new coping habits are learned. Failure to use vacation or leisure time to learn new coping skills accounts for an almost immediate loss of benefits when returning back to work or home. Here are some antidepression strategies that might help you deal with everyday, "garden-variety" depression. These are general approaches.

1. You can increase activation or arousal level by sensory, physical, and mental stimulation. Breaks in routine provide novel stimulation and increase energy. Increasing stress through activity produces the energy necessary to cope with the situations causing depression.

2. Behavioral structuring will help you develop behavioral objectives that are attainable and will ultimately lead to resolving the problem or achieving a goal. Adaptive goal setting will restore the perceived relationship between your behavior and its rewards. You will perceive that your behaviors are effective in producing results, and the good feeling of achieving will produce more energy.

3. Highlight your successes. Write successes down and review your list. Kick false modesty in the pants. I want to remind you that one of the characteristics of coronary-prone people is that they do not get any joy out of their accomplishments. Use your success to support more constructive mental-sets that enhance self-esteem.

PREVENTING DEPRESSION

Although it is impossible to avoid all depression, there are some general strategies that are useful for avoiding serious depression.

First, you can learn to control emotional responses by having the opportunity to deal with stressors under the guidance of another experienced person. Friends and relatives are often helpful in this way. A history of shared mastery experiences throughout the development of an individual's life seems to "inoculate" against future depression. A powerful type of learning called *modeling* underlies stress inoculation. Modeling is learning new or modifying existing behaviors by observing the behaviors of others. Much to the horror of parents, children mimic the voice and gestures of a parent who has punished them. When children are punished, they learn how to punish. Parents also are models for coping with stress. Children acquire many of their adult coping behaviors by observing how parents solve and emotionally respond to problems. Adults model the behaviors of those who are emotionally tied to them. It is helpful to change or avoid relationships with people who are always depressed, angry, or cynical. There is a well-known psychiatric disorder called *folie à deux* (madness of two), in which one person's insanity is acquired and shared by another who is emotionally close.

DEPRESSION AND PROBLEM SOLVING

There are at least three possible consequences of depression that affect our ability to solve problems. All are dependent upon arousal level. During the elevated arousal levels of agitated depression, we might suffer a restriction of perceived alternative solutions. Secondly, it is possible to experience an overload or flooding of nonproductive cues, which lead to nonproductive behaviors. Finally, the low arousal of some types of depression produces a deficit of stress energy and a halfhearted consideration of alternative solutions. Motor depression is difficult to overcome because of the lack of energy to initiate coping responses. It is difficult to face the tasks of a new day with reluctance and a shortage of energy. The tendency to stay in bed and call in sick or, better yet, to have someone else call in for us can be almost overwhelming. But after forcing ourselves to dress and go to work, we begin to feel better. The stimulation of our effort produces energy to work and get rid of depression. If positive thinking is added to that, we might have a truly exceptional day.

SHARPENING DISCRIMINATION

Learned-helplessness-sets contribute to a breakdown in the ability to perceive that escape from an unpleasant situation is possible. If past experiences have taught us that our behaviors are not related to rewards or punishments, then escape is not attempted even if it is possible. Negative expectations paralyze the ability to discriminate between threatening and nonthreatening situations. If we feel that we are generally treated unjustly, then there is an inclination to interpret all events in that light. The "Why try? I'll get in trouble anyway" type of thinking impairs rational assessment of reality. People who have learned maladaptive discrimination skills are often described by friends as always being angry, fearful, or depressed. If you find yourself feeling that way, make an effort to set aside negative feelings. Examine each situation objectively, as if it were a new one.

DEPRESSION AND DIET

We know that neurotransmitter deficits can cause depression and that depressive learning situations can cause neurotransmitter deficits. We also know that the blood levels of some neurotransmitters are dependent upon daily food intake. It is important to eat three meals a day. Do not overeat. Reduce the amount of food per meal if you add an additional meal during the day, and eat a variety of healthy foods. Also, try to keep sugar intake down. It is all too common to hear about the "I can't eat a thing in the morning; I just have coffee" diet. The caffeine in the coffee promotes hypoglycemia, then comes the midmorning donut or candy bar, which leads to more sugar imbalance. There is little food value in junk foods, and even the substances required by the body to manufacture neurotransmitters are often absent. Poor eating habits can be expected to bring a slump in energy, a dull headache, and depression in the afternoon.

PHYSICAL EXERCISE
Instead of a coffee break, some businesses provide morning and afternoon exercise breaks. Music is played over the intercom and employees meet in a large area to exercise together. Breaks also provide social interaction, which is helpful in reducing monotony. Employees report feeling more energized and fresh throughout the day. Unfortunately when it comes to exercise, as a nation we are laggards. Fewer than 50 percent of Americans exercise regularly. Although the old saying "A healthy body, a healthy mind" is an overstatement (I've seen quite a few physically healthy neurotics), there is little doubt that regular physical exercise is necessary to maintain good health. Regular exercise increases muscle tone and enhances performance. Muscles are more prepared to respond. More sensations flow to the brain, raising arousal level and generating more energy. One good thing about exercise is that it is an easily scheduled activity that produces immediate results. This is one of the reasons why reports of mood improvements with exercise are so common.

DEPRESSION AND SLEEP
Sleep and waking patterns are critical to the maintenance of optimal stress-energy levels. Waking in the middle of the night is frequently a sign of depression. The effects of "jet lag" are commonly experienced because of a disruption in circadian rhythms, in this case, the biochemical and bioelectrical cycles that relate to sleep. Shift work is another culprit. Frequent alternating between morning and night shifts disrupts bodily cycles, and neurotransmitters are secreted at levels inadequate for either sleep or work. There is an ave-

raging out of the transmitters underlying arousal level and, hence, energy declines. Depression is a common complaint of both travelers and shift workers. The amount of sleep needed varies from person to person.

If you awaken refreshed and rested in the morning, then you are probably getting enough sleep. Heavy coffee drinkers frequently report little difficulty in getting to sleep and also sleep through the night without awakening. Their sleep, however, is often robbed of some of its benefits.

BIORHYTHMS

Hormonal, biochemical, temperature, bioelectrical, and behavioral cycles are critical to changes in our moods. These rhythms are complex and interrelated. Biorhythm systems that are based upon the date of birth and claim to be able to predict intellectual and emotional highs and lows have no scientific basis. One reason that the predictions based on these cycles occasionally seem to be valid is that they provide the basis for self-fulfilling prophecies. If a chart shows that low emotional and intellectual cycles coincide, then what is experienced is what is expected.

RELAXATION

True relaxation, the complete physical relaxation of the body, is helpful in replenishing energy resources during the day. This will help reduce depression as well as improve performance. Chapter 5 describes a number of relaxation exercises.

UNSOLVABLE PROBLEMS

Finally, some problems *cannot* be solved. In those cases, adapt—accept that there are some things over which you exert little control. Avoid overcontrolling and overgeneralizing from your disappointments.

PHYSICAL AND PSYCHOLOGICAL
EFFECTS OF BOREDOM

Stimulation coming from our internal and external environments keeps us active by placing demands upon our nervous system which in turn produce energy. Frequent presentation of a given stimulus reduces the nervous system's response to it. Our nervous system's response declines unless we have labeled that stimulus as being important. We have the ability to define even the most repetitive and monotonous task as interesting to keep our stress at levels optimal for performance.

Researchers interested in human performance have found that monotonous tasks produce boredom. Boredom reduces productivity and increases tension and anxiety. Tension and anxiety are correlated with physical and psychological problems. Monotony might lead to such consequences, but not necessarily. People often perform repetitive tasks under conditions of low environmental or intellectual stimulation without feeling bored. Some have made those activities stimulating by labeling them as interesting or at least as being important to them.

There is a tendency to label situations that require repetitive effort or are beyond our control as boring. College students sometimes become sleepy when they begin reading required homework assignments, but snap back to life when they are asked to go out for a beer.

Feelings of being entrapped are common in marital relationships. Either the husband or wife feels trapped, anxious, and bored. Boredom leads to tension and depression. Sexual interest declines and ultimately an argument occurs. Initially, the increases in stress energy generated by the argument might reawaken the couple's interest in each other and, hence, we see the "fight, kiss, and make up" pattern. After a while, however, that also becomes a no-control situation—"All we do is fight all of the time"—which is boring, and either chronic lack of interest becomes a way of life or the intensity of the frustration is converted to anger and is released in physical violence.

FATIGUE VERSUS BOREDOM

Fatigue and boredom are not the same. Fatigue is a complex psychophysiological state that builds during periods of physical or psychological demand, because some of the body's resources have been partially expended. Boredom is a type of psychological fatigue that arises from perceptions of monotony or disinterest. Our energy quickly returns when we turn away from a boring task. We might, however, become fatigued while doing something that is interesting to us and then need to rest.

Bodily resources are generally ample during boredom; therefore, energy resources are not lacking, but are not used for the task. Energy can be channeled into tension and anxiety. Just the opposite can also happen. Once a task or stimulus is labeled as boring, the brain has the ability to suppress or inhibit its function. It can decrease the arousal level of the entire body. The result is feeling drowsy. One of the most embarrassing outcomes can be falling asleep while listening to someone talk. This suppression is partially under control of our attention mechanism. When we hear or see a stimulus that we have defined and labeled as important, we attend to it. Similarly, there are situations and people that turn us off. When we are no longer confronted with them, our energy returns.

LEISURE TIME AND BOREDOM

A common misunderstanding is that leisure time means idleness. Activity and stimulation are necessary for physical and psychological well-being. I have observed a pattern of behavior that I call the "college student summer syndrome." It applies, however, to others as well. In some cases where students have not found summer employment and there is no compelling reason for them to get out of bed in the morning, they begin going to bed later at night and sleeping later during the day. This disrupts sleep-waking patterns. The days slip by and perhaps TV-watching becomes the prime activity. Eating may increase and take on the characteristics of grazing. Soon chronic fatigue develops. Cognitive-sets change to "life is boring." Self-esteem declines and the person feels a lack of purpose, incompetent, or socially awkward. Leisure time, to be of value, requires some planning. Time for rest and activities should be flexibly scheduled. Setting leisure-time objectives provides an opportunity to exercise control over activities that are perceived as pleasant. This strengthens perceptions of control. Don't develop the itinerary of a recreation director aboard a cruise ship, but simply identify an activity and rest period for each significant period of leisure time. The apathy and boredom of "time on your hands" can be just as dangerous as overwork.

OVERCOMING BOREDOM

Boredom is to a large degree a learned mental state. A great variety of activities or situations are labeled as boring by some and not boring by others. Task intricacy and monotony do not totally cause boredom. It is true that the nervous system reduces its response to familiar or repetitive stimuli, but that alone is not enough to account for boredom. It is not the task that is boring in itself, but how we label it—something to be kept in mind while reading the following suggestions for overcoming boredom.

Increase feelings of control. Feelings of being trapped or lacking control over our responses and environments can lead to boredom. The frustration of thinking that we must perform a boring task generates energy. In many of these situations, energy is channeled into nonproductive emotions. Too much energy is produced to do the job. Think of a task that you did not want to do, but felt that you had no choice. You will probably recall being irritated, which made the effort more difficult. In the majority of life situations it is important to remember that you can always make choices and, in that sense, are always in control. If your work is boring for you, then you have several categories of choice. You can possibly find another job, shift jobs within the organization, or change your current working conditions.

An assembly-line worker told me that he hated his job and disliked going to work every day. I asked him why he continued working there. He said that it paid good money. He blamed the management for his unhappiness and was an unhealthy, underproductive worker. It was really *his* decision to stay. He had not thought about the alternatives open to him to improve his own situation. Chronic discontent is a self-destructive habit.

Occasionally, take a moment out of your day to review the possibilities of choice available to you in work or home environments. Talking with someone is helpful in generating alternatives. Realizing that there are choices and that you are choosing will increase feelings of control and reduce boredom.

Learn to persevere. How many times have you heard the easily given advice "Hang in there—stick with it"? The problem is that no one tells us how to learn how to persevere. One way is through a self-contract. Write down your work-load objectives and the rewards that will follow their accomplishment. This can be done on the basis of time spent or work completed. You might set an objective for five work units and then schedule a break. Break activities should be rewarding. If they are, they will reinforce work behavior. I favor the number of work units produced as the determinant of self-reward. Examples of some different work units are number of pages read, letters written, parts assembled, pounds lost by dieting, or tasks completed.

Relate efforts to rewards. You should ask, "Why am I doing this?" whenever you experience boredom. If the answer does not come quickly into mind, stop and mentally rehearse the ultimate benefits of your activity. You might be extrinsically motivated by money, praise, or physical comfort, or you may be intrinsically motivated by feelings of accomplishment or creativity. Whatever the reason, keep it in mind and relate your efforts to that end. If you cannot think of any benefits, then it is time to exercise your choice and find some other activity.

All of these antiboredom strategies require effort on your part. You might initially have to learn some skills to generate enough energy to reduce boredom as well as learn how to divert stress energy into behaviors that are productive. Research shows us what can happen when boredom is uncontrolled—high adrenaline secretion, inability to relax even after work is finished, and increased danger of developing psychosomatic disease.

II: ANXIETY INTO ENERGY

5: LEARNING HOW TO RELAX

Tension stress is an unwelcome guest that cannot always be avoided. Little annoyances build slowly during the day and escape unnoticed. Suddenly, we are beyond the range of our stress window and stress is no longer a friend. Stress also may increase gradually over longer periods of time, exceeding the optimal range of our stress window. This chapter offers a variety of simple, but effective relaxation techniques.

RELAXATION IS NOT DISTRACTION

Most people have not learned how to relax. When I am lecturing, I often ask members of the audience how they relax. Common responses are running, playing tennis, golfing, going on vacation, and having two, three, or four martinis. These activities are not relaxation—the martinis are sedation. They require an energy response from the body that creates stress. That statement often raises the hackles of the joggers in the crowd. They will argue that while they are running they feel great. Their worries seem to evaporate.

Nevertheless, that is not relaxation; that is distraction. When we do something that we really enjoy, even if it is stressful, problems and worries are forgotten. We are granted a reprieve from our usual stressors. We thrive on variety and change, provided that we perceive that we control them. Our recreational activities are necessary to nourish healthy physical and psychological states. After jogging or golfing, we may relax, and that is good.

WHAT IS RELAXATION?

Relaxation is the achievement and maintenance of physiological and psychological states of calm. Activity in the nervous system becomes more rhythmic. Muscle tone decreases and generally we say that the autonomic nervous system, which controls our heart and other organs, switches over to a parasympathetic or "relax" mode. The body conserves, repairs, and restores its energy.

It is important to acquire mastery of the skill of relaxation. Relaxation, then, becomes a "controlled" ability. Knowledge that you have the power to relax whenever you wish is knowledge that you are in control of tension. At any time, in any situation, you can relax. As you read through these exercises, place a check beside the ones that sound reasonable and interesting to you. Obviously, in the middle of a meeting, you cannot lie on the floor and begin to tense your muscle groups progressively. Select one or two techniques and begin to practice daily. Probably the best scheduling rule is to practice each exercise at least once each day. Two times would be better. Set aside a time each day for practice. If you miss that time, however, don't give up. Simply work your practice in during some other part of the day.

Some of these exercises will produce immediate results.

Others will require a little practice before they begin to pay off. All of these relaxation skills will yield an increase in benefits with practice. Before you try a particular exercise, measure your tension level. One useful way to do this is to assign your feeling of tension a score from 0 to 100. Let 0 represent the most relaxed you have ever been and 100 the most stressed you have ever been. Write your score down and then measure your tension level after completing the exercise. Write that down also and keep a daily record. This will allow you to measure quantitatively the effectiveness of both the type of relaxation technique and the effects of your practice.

BREATHING EXERCISE

Breathing patterns are often affected by tension and anxiety. Breathing may become more rapid and shallow under increased tension stress. Hyperventilation, rapid and deep respiration leading to an excessive loss of carbon dioxide from the blood, may also occur. This exercise concentrates upon achieving deep and regular breathing. It may be practiced at almost any time or place throughout the day.

1. Slowly draw a deep breath. Try to expand your rib cage as much as possible.
2. Hold your breath for approximately five seconds.
3. Release your breath slowly while saying the word *relax* to yourself as you do.
4. Repeat steps 1 through 3 at least five times.

I prefer using the word *relax*. One obvious reason is related to the meaning of the word itself; the other reason is that the word *relax* is also used in the progressive muscle exercise. With practice the word *relax* itself becomes a signal for relaxation.

PROGRESSIVE MUSCLE EXERCISE

Before beginning this exercise, at least for the first few times, select a relatively quiet, comfortable environment where you will not be disturbed. Be creative in your search for a relaxation hideout. One of my former seminar participants uses the back seat of his car during his lunch hour. Others have put "Do Not Disturb" signs on storerooms in the office.

1. Loosen any tight clothing. Untie or remove your shoes. I prefer to take my shoes off. Also remove any jewelry that might be uncomfortable for you.

2. Close your eyes and perform the breathing exercise described above. The breathing exercise is not necessary, but it often enhances relaxation. Pairing the two also strengthens the breathing exercise so that it is more effective when used alone during the day.

3. Follow the steps below to tense and relax key muscle groups of the body. Tighten each muscle group until you become aware of a moderate degree of muscle tension.

4. Hold the tension for approximately five seconds; then relax slowly saying "relax" to yourself. If cramping should occur in some muscles, reduce the intensity of the contraction. Also avoid tensing parts of the body that may have been injured. After tensing a muscle group, repeat the same exercise so that you do each exercise twice.

SEQUENCE OF MUSCLE CONTRACTION AND RELAXATION

Toes, legs, thighs

1. Curl the toes downward, release, say "relax" to yourself.

2. Curl the toes upward.

3. Tense the muscles in both legs by making them rigid.

4. Tense the muscles in your thighs.

5. Relax toes, legs, and thighs. Imagine that they are warm and heavy.

Stomach, back, shoulders

1. Tense your stomach by pushing out with your stomach muscles, as if you were preparing to be hit in the stomach. Don't forget to say "relax" to yourself as you release the tension each time.

2. Pull your stomach inward as far as you can.

3. Arch your back as much as possible without causing pain or soreness. The muscles of the lower back are especially sensitive to tension. If cramping occurs, reduce the amount of tension you are creating.

4. Bring your shoulders forward as if you are going to try to touch them together.

5. Move your shoulders back as far as you can, hold for about five seconds, saying "relax" to yourself as you release the tension.

6. Relax your stomach, back, shoulders. Breathe deeply and go on to the next set of exercises.

Fingers, hands, arms, neck

1. Spread your fingers far apart until you feel tension in your hands.

2. Make a fist by clenching your hands tightly.

3. Tense both arms and hold them out in front of you.

4. Bend your head down and try to touch your chin to your chest.

5. Bend your head back as far as possible.

6. Now relax your fingers, hands, arms, and neck.

Face, eyes

1. Make a face by squinting your eyes and tightening up the muscles of your cheeks and mouth.

2. Raise your eyebrows and wrinkle your forehead.

3. Slowly move your eyes around in a circle, first one way and then the other.

When you have finished this sequence, relax all of the muscles of your body. Breathe deeply, slowly count to five, and open your eyes. Orient yourself to the room and slowly get up.

AUTOHYPNOSIS

Some people have reported that autohypnosis is useful in combating insomnia. A small night-light, clock, or luminous paint dot is used to replace the fixation dot mentioned in step 1 if you wish to use this technique at night.

1. Select a comfortable chair or bed. Place a dot or cross on the wall at eye level.

2. Complete the breathing exercise mentioned earlier in this chapter (see page 87).

3. Count backward from ten, taking a deep breath and releasing slowly for each number.

4. Try to imagine that your arms and legs are becoming heavy and warm.

5. Close your eyes and count forward to ten, slowly drawing a deep breath for every count.

6. When you reach ten use your imagination to visualize a scene that is pleasant or peaceful. Relax all of your muscles and breathe deeply.

Many of those who try this exercise fall asleep before they get to step 5. I do want to remind you, however, that falling asleep is not learning how to relax. If relaxation is your goal, you should avoid sleeping. After meals, just after rising, and just before going to bed are not the best times to practice relaxation skills because there is a greater tendency to sleep.

DESENSITIZATION

Most of us function rather well most of the time, but there is that one activity, object, situation, or person that raises our tension level. Desensitization is a learning technique that reduces the tension-producing power of a specific stimulus and replaces it with a relaxation response. Imagine relaxing when you go to see the boss rather than suffering from excessive tension.

1. Specifically identify the stressor that increases your tension level to an unacceptable level.

2. On index cards write four to seven brief paragraphs about the tension-producing stimulus. Write each paragraph so that each successive description elicits more tension. You must use imagination to develop these descriptions. For example, the target situation and activity might be speaking before a group. The first paragraph might describe an empty classroom that could be used for public speaking, but you imagine it to be empty and really do not have to speak there. You are just walking around this room to become familiar with it. Paragraph 2, then, might include a description of the empty room, but you imagine that you will be speaking there in a month or so. Paragraph 3 could be a description of the room filled with people, but you are not there to speak. The last description would include you speaking before a group in that room.

3. Arrange the cards in order from the least tension producing to the most tension producing.

4. Relax by using the breathing exercise or the progressive muscle exercise on page 88.

5. Before starting with card 1, scale your tension level by assigning a value from 0 (completely relaxed) to 100 (the most tense you have ever been).

6. Using your imagination, try to realize the scenes described on card 1. If you begin to become tense, take a deep breath, hold it for three to five seconds, release it slowly, and say "relax" to yourself. Rate your tension level again if necessary to be sure that you are as relaxed as you were when you started. When you can successfully imagine the scene on card 1 without an increase in tension, go on to card

2. Continue working through the scenes on each successive card until you have achieved an acceptable level of tension on the last and most threatening card.

7. Work through your cards at least once a day for ten days. Measure your progress by comparing your tension level before you began desensitization. It may be necessary to continue practicing for another ten days or even more. But if a few minutes a day spent for a few days helps you reduce tension stress, it will be worth the work.

Unwelcome thoughts can spoil physical relaxation. The next two relaxation techniques involve the use of your imagination to achieve a peaceful mental state. They fall under the category of imagery or fantasy training. I recommend that you use one of the more physical relaxation methods already discussed before you try imagery relaxation.

MENTAL RELAXATION

1. Begin with breathing, progressive relaxation, or any other technique that helps you to relax physically. Allow your mind to become passive. Let the ideas flow freely in and out of your mind.

2. If a worrying thought occurs, try saying no under your breath to block it. Some of my clients say that as soon as they say no, they have even more difficulty blocking the unwanted thought. In that case, just take a deep breath and say "relax" to yourself.

3. Imagine a scene that is peaceful and pleasant for you. It could be an image of lying on a beach with the sound of the surf breaking—the warm sun on

your back. Try to picture and sense the details of your scene vividly.

4. After a while, concentrate on your slow and deep breathing. As you release each breath, say "relax" to yourself.

BEHAVIORAL REHEARSAL

Psychologist Donald Meichenbaum has developed a behavioral rehearsal drill. This drill allows you to use your imagination to work through an anticipated stressful experience mentally. You think of the stressful situation and imagine how you would confront it. Couple this with relaxation training and you will effectively reduce the tension-producing effects of that situation.

1. Identify and describe a specific stressful situation. For example, "I have to meet with an Internal Revenue Service representative for an income-tax audit on Friday at 2:00 P.M."

2. Identify the psychological and physical tension-stress reactions that you are apt to experience.

3. List several alternative ways to deal with your tension stress, for example, breathing exercises, progressive relaxation, or taking a hot bath.

4. Develop a schedule and plan of action. When will you do your relaxation exercises? There are some organizational activities that might be done beforehand. For an income-tax audit, it might be to organize your receipts and to develop a plan to give yourself plenty of time to get to your appointment.

5. Use your imagination to rehearse the meeting. Imagine sitting across from the auditor and breathe deeply, saying "relax" to yourself if you begin to experience tension stress.

6. After the actual event has taken place, review your performance. Highlight your successes. Look to see where you might improve your handling of similar situations for the future.

The techniques that have been discussed thus far are useful and effective for reducing tension stress. Although they certainly help, they do not solve the complex problems that often cause tension stress. The comprehensive Individual Stress-Management Program that follows represents the application of an old and well-known problem-solving model to managing stress. This program is used to change a lifestyle that generates excessive tension stress.

A firm commitment to change is an absolute prerequisite to beginning a stress-management program. Stress reactions are learned patterns of behavior that are laid down like bricks in a wall over the entire span of life. It will take considerable patience and effort to dismantle the wall of tension-stress reaction patterns that you have built throughout your life. It is best to begin this task thoughtfully and slowly. Do not use the sledgehammer technique—trying to knock the whole wall down in one or two weeks. Your stress-management program would best be described as a persistent, orchestrated effort to achieve an optimal level of stress, and this will require a realistic commitment to stick with your program before you begin.

FOUR BASIC STEPS OF STRESS MANAGEMENT AND PROBLEM SOLVING

AWARENESS (A)

Unhealthy stress patterns are often difficult to identify. Over time we become adapted or accustomed to heightened stress states. Although the physiological processes underlying sensory adaptation are somewhat different, sensory adaptation provides us with an analogy of how we can lose awareness of meaningful stimuli. Everyone has had the experience of having to check to see whether he is wearing a ring or watch and is surprised that the item is there or, sometimes, that it is not there. When we draw water for a bath, how many of us have tested the water with our hand, thinking that more hot water should be added, and more yet? Then when the bath feels just right, we jump in and cook everything from the waist down! Adaptation to tension stress occurs in a similar way. Our stress-response levels can gradually increase over time so that we are unaware of how stressed we are. Furthermore, we tend to deny that our tension-stress levels have increased.

Techniques to increase awareness. Raising our level of awareness of tension stress is often difficult and not only requires new information about the nature of stress but also bodily experiences. Many of the elements of the stress-management program are designed to increase both physiological and psychological awareness of stress and stressors. One simple way to increase awareness is to keep a daily journal for one or two weeks to record the stressors and your stress reactions to them. Another technique that has been used by behavioral psychologists to measure changes in behavior is to pick one or two stressors and stress reactions and count the number of times that they occur for a given two-week period.

NATURE

Sources of stress. A stressor is any stimulus, thing, place, person, thought, or event that places some demand upon you either physically or psychologically. If you try to list stressors that are important for you, these are some of the life areas that should be considered: work, sex, marriage, finances, interpersonal relationships, meeting deadlines, doing a good job, meeting new people, talking in front of groups or strangers, physical problems (health), dealing with new situations, competitive situations, physical appearance, and understimulating environments.

Stress reactions. The following are common stress reactions and can help you identify your responses to stressors. The stress indicators listed in chapter 1 and all of the self-tests in this book will be useful to you, too.

Physiological reactions include headaches, hands perspiring, sexual difficulties, increased heart rate, fluttery feeling in stomach, weight loss or gain, constipation or diarrhea, hands shaking, excessive perspiration, rapid breathing.

Psychological responses are depression, anxiety, changing self-concept, loss of confidence, feelings of strain, feelings of helplessness or hopelessness, excessive concern about the future, anger, frustration, boredom.

Behavioral signals may be aggression, difficulty in making up your mind, restlessness and inability to relax, sleep problems, interpersonal problems, hyperactivity, nail biting.

I have given more emphasis to the first step, awareness, because it is most important in learning how to use your stress energy productively. Awareness is a learned skill that must be practiced to become a life-long aid.

IDENTIFICATION (I) OF STRESS OR STRESSOR PROBLEMS

Once you begin increasing your awareness of stress and stressors, you will find it helpful to write down the specific problems that you are able to identify. Associating specific situations or people with your own stress responses will help you move on to the next step, management.

MANAGEMENT (M) OF STRESSORS AND STRESS REACTIONS

You will find it useful to take each problem listed in the preceding step and to "brainstorm" as many alternative solutions as possible. Then, for each alternative, write down all of the resources available to you to help solve that problem. Behavioral action plans will involve changing your response, changing the things around you, or both. Once you have worked this far, go back over your lists and choose the most beneficial plan of action. You can assign plusses and minuses to alternatives to help you assess the costs and benefits of each alternative. Develop a time schedule, if necessary, to make sure that you follow your plan. When you begin implementing your plan, you are ready for the last step—self-evaluation.

SELF-EVALUATION (S)

Programs are meant to be flexible. Periodically assessing the effectiveness of your program will provide you with feedback information to make improvements. The general rule in making program changes is to change only *one* thing at a time and give that enough time to prove its effectiveness. Knowledge of your own success will reinforce you to continue your efforts. Enjoy your successes, share them with others, and reward yourself for achieving your objectives.

Put the first letter of each step above together and you find the acronym *AIMS.* AIMS is a rational approach to living that requires some time and effort but helps channel valuable stress energy into effective, efficient, and, hopefully, more healthy living.

HOW TO SET GOALS AND OBJECTIVES

After working through AIMS, you are ready to arrange a schedule and plan of action systematically. The following should help you develop your program.

1. Identify specific behavioral objectives. These are specific coping behaviors directed toward environmental change or habit change, for example, eliminating noise in the workplace by requesting an office change, losing a certain amount of weight by dieting, or practicing a progressive muscle exercise a certain number of times per week to help control tension.

2. Establish behavioral milestones or subgoals. These will be specific actions or end products that lead to your objectives, for example, reducing the number of cigarettes smoked by four the first week, four more the next week, and so on.

3. Set target dates to correspond to the realistic completion or attainment of the milestones.

As you develop your stress-management program, try to set realistic goals and objectives. Excessively ambitious objectives lead to failure, which increases tension, self-blame, and helplessness. On the other hand, objectives that are too easily attained do not enhance self-concept or lead to meaningful results.

There are many other relaxation techniques that might be effective for you. Some have a religious or mystical flavor; others come from research; and some are quite simple, for example, sitting in a comfortable chair and listening to some relaxing music. What really counts is that you begin learning a rational, systematic approach, such as AIMS, to control your stress energy resources. That is the long-run and lasting effort that will help you the most.

6: FINDING YOUR STRESS WINDOW

How much stress is too much stress? How do you know whether you are functioning in the realm of your stress window? The stress window is a holistic concept relating to the total functioning and state of the individual. It is optimal physical, emotional, motivational, and cognitive functioning. The energy produced and experienced when we are operating in the region of our stress window is adaptive stress. It is beneficial to our survival. Unfortunately, too many of us only operate through our stress window occasionally. Stress energy is often underproduced, overproduced, or misdirected.

Physical and psychological individual differences influence the location of the stress window. It is different for each of us. Our physical condition is dependent upon heredity, diet, exercise, rest, environmental conditions, and history of bodily injury and disease. If people are subjected to an intense chronic stressor, after a while they will become exhausted. Physical exhaustion occurs at different rates for different people because of their unique physical makeup, experience, and mental-sets.

Stress, motivational, cognitive, emotional, and physical

dynamics contribute to our feelings of well-being. Learning to function within your stress window will not be achieved overnight. Because of the uniqueness of each of us, each will need to proceed at his or her own rate of learning and ability to practice. For this reason, I have avoided developing a program based on a certain number of days and would strongly advise against most of those programs that do. You must identify, select, and schedule your own coping behaviors according to the *realistic* demands of your situation. The goal of every individualized program of change should be to develop coping skills that produce results. Your efforts must be seen as being effective. This will help prevent feelings of helplessness and help build feelings of perceived control and self-esteem.

Learning to function in your stress window aids in accomplishing the tasks of the moment, but more permanent advantages will also come your way. Long-term physiological and psychological changes occur. They strengthen you to meet the consequences of too little or too much stress that might occur in the future. The process of functioning in your stress window is dependent upon learning and personal growth.

Although you can look to others for suggestions to feel and perform well, you must take control and make the critical decisions for action. Reliance upon others to make decisions for you and the use of drugs to cope with understimulation or overstimulation and the resulting stress cause feelings of helplessness and perceptions of lack of control. Sometimes well-meaning advice motivates attempts of overcontrol, that is, trying to control the uncontrollable. That leads to failure.

AN INVENTORY OF YOUR MENTAL SETS

Cognitive strategies or mental-sets are important in finding
your stress window. As we have seen, thoughts can and do
control physiology. Mental-sets are learned gradually. As
they are developed, they in turn shape our experience of
the present and expectations for the future. Because sets
develop slowly, they may escape our awareness. Discover-
ing and using your stress window involves in part discover-
ing and creating new sets and destroying old ones. Try to
identify the sets that are currently operating in your life.
Some common negative mental sets include: fear of the
future or anticipation of what might be; distrust of people;
feelings of helplessness, anger, bitterness, and fatigue; and
beliefs of self-righteousness or authoritarianism. Maladaptive social attitudes seen in prejudice frequently represent
displacements of anger and frustration to easily identifiable
groups or issues. Unfortunately, this type of release generates more tension and is self-destructive. Psychologies that
favor the selfish attitude of "putting other people in their
place" are destructive. Self-esteem should always flow out
of positive feelings of what you are able to accomplish for
yourself or others, not from striking out against others. Competition is a healthy process of recognizing your own growth
by comparing your achievement with that of others. Chronic
competitive-sets, however, foster excessive conflict and
maladaptive behavioral patterns. Chronic worry about win-
ning or about defeating an opponent creates a tension-stress
physiology. Feelings of accomplishment and personal
growth generate adaptive-stress energy

POSITIVE MENTAL SETS

Positive mental-sets include perceptions of control; feelings
of competency, confidence, interest, and high self-esteem;
trust in people and in the future; and recognition that you
have the energy necessary to achieve realistic goals. Posi-

tive sets concentrate your awareness on strengths and accomplishments and help you avoid overcontrolling the
events and people that are important. I would recommend
that you sit for a few minutes during a quiet time. List and
describe the mental sets that are operating in your life. Place
a check mark next to those sets that are negative and cause
anxiety or worry. Underline your positive sets; they are powerful resources.

HOW TO FIND YOUR STRESS WINDOW

In earlier chapters, tests were provided to help you assess
stress and tension, perception of control, and depression.
The tension-stress score reflects physical, behavioral, emotional, and motivational aspects of stress. The perceived
control score is an individualized measurement of your general feelings of control. The individual depression scale
measures physical, emotional, motivational, and cognitive
elements of depression. By plotting these test scores on the
Stress-Window Profile, you will be able to determine
whether you are operating in the realm of your stress window. If a score falls outside of the window, it will identify the
general area where new skills need to be learned. This is a
conservative estimate of functioning, which means that if
you score within the stress window, you are not suffering
from excessive tension stress. There is, of course, always
room for improvement. That is growth. You might still feel
some tension or anxiety, but they most likely are normal
physiological or psychological signs of living. Falling within
the stress window provides an opportunity to use your stress
energy to enhance living.

Before continuing to discuss the significance of scores
falling outside of the stress window, I want to pass along a
rule of thumb that I first heard during a personality course
I took many years ago: "If you want to know what is bother-

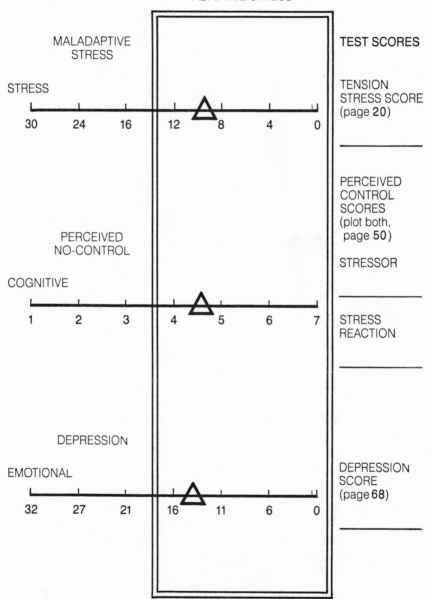

$\triangle$= Average score for subjects taking tests

FIGURE 3   STRESS-WINDOW PROFILE

ing a person, just ask him." This statement was made in reference to the excessive use of psychological testing. I have found it to be very useful and timesaving in helping clients pinpoint problems. You might be one of those people who knows that you are functioning well or where your problems lie. If so, it is not necessary to work through all of the tests and plot your stress-window profile. The only caution is that you watch out for those slow-developing problems that creep up and distort your self-awareness. The most tense individuals are often the ones to deny that they have tension problems. If you have considered that possibility thoroughly and have eliminated chronic tension stress, no-control perceptions, and depression as serious influences in your life, then you can dispense with the testing and consider some of the other suggestions to increase your awareness of good stress that follow in this chapter or go on to the next chapter to consider some of the ways to generate stress energy.

WHAT DO MALADAPTIVE STRESS-WINDOW SCORES MEAN?

The word *maladaptive* does not necessarily mean that disease or emotional problems exist or are inevitable. It means that behaviors might not be constructive or productive in dealing with stress or environments—they are not adaptive. I will describe some of the possible interpretations of test scores that fall outside the area of the stress window.

Tension-Stress test. A tension-stress score of 13 or above indicates that you have a tension-stress management problem, that is, anxiety is a problem for you. If perceived control and depression scores, however, are within the stress window and your tension score outside, it is most likely that you have not learned how to relax. The relaxation skills offered in chapter 5 will help you. A high tension-stress score tells us something about our environment as well as how we perceive it. Understimulating and overstimulating environments as extremes lead to tension stress and anxiety. Chapter 4 suggests some ways to deal with boredom, which is one consequence of understimulation or environments that have been defined as understimulating. Paradoxically, understimulation and a lack of activity sometimes produce excessive tension. In those cases, stress energy must be channeled into constructive activity. In cases of hypoactivity, stress energy should be generated to get us moving again.

Perceived Control Scale. If you have read earlier chapters, you know that the consequences of perceiving that you are not generally in control of your own stress responses or the events that influence your life cause the secretion of excessive amounts of adrenaline and other stress hormones to overdrive the body's physiology. In addition, mental-sets of helplessness develop that can lead to depression or further increases in anxiety. The perceived control scores that you have plotted on your stress-window profile are unique because they reflect your own assessment of how you perceive your control over the stressors and stress reactions operating in your life. If either of your perceived control scores falls outside the stress window, you should ask yourself these questions:

1. Is the stressor really important to me?

2. In how many different ways can I effectively deal with it?

3. What resources do I have to reduce the impact of the stress reaction or stressor?

4. Can either the stressor or stress reaction be controlled?

5. Am I attempting to overcontrol?

All too often, relatively insignificant matters become perceived as being more stress producing or important than they really should be. Normally small events can become tied into our general stress response and raise it to a point where perception is distorted.

A friend of mine went to see a film, was delayed in traffic, and feared that he would be late. His activation level was elevated because of his worry and rush to get to the theater in time. He bought his ticket and found a seat. Soon, two people sat in front of him and began talking loudly. One of them had already seen the film and was telling the other what was going to happen. My friend moved to a new seat, which was not quite as choice, and watched the film. That should have been enough, but he was too upset to enjoy the film. After the film was over, he could only talk about the rudeness of the people who sat in front of him and how *they* had spoiled the film. It was really a simple matter of moving to a new seat or asking the people to be quiet. The stress of rushing to the theater combined with a ''people are no damned good'' set produced stress energy far beyond that called for to meet the coping demands of changing seats. The inconsiderate behavior of others became more important than the film. In a case such as this, it is essential to remember what is important and what is not. With very few exceptions, we are the ones who have made the decision to remain in a given situation. No one forces us to stay. We choose to stay. We must remind ourselves now and then that we always have a choice. We must gain a perspective on our situation. Discrimination can be sharpened by taking the event out of context and evaluating it in itself. Control! Do not let the amount of stress energy generated get out of hand. This is your responsibility, not someone else's.

ACCEPT IT—THAT IS EASY TO SAY

If a stressor is labeled as important, then as many alternative coping responses as possible should be considered along

with the resources available. If your best efforts are not effective, then it is best to accept that you have no control over
that stressor. That is easy to say, but not always easy to do,
unless you have learned how to relax or control your tension
levels. Although you have told yourself that you cannot control a stressor and therefore should not worry, nagging
thoughts and emotions might linger. Under these conditions, it is necessary for you to use your relaxation skills. They
will reduce your tension-stress level, which will help you
accept the situation and put it behind you. Failure to do this
will land you right into the middle of an overcontrol-set. You
will generate and expend energy that will not produce
adaptive results simply because the stressor is beyond your
control. Learned helplessness, tension stress, and anxiety
are the maladaptive consequences. Accepting that you do
not have control over a stressor is an active decision-making
process. It is not running away. In many cases, it takes more
strength and courage to admit to yourself that a thing is
beyond your control than to continue wearing yourself
down.

Individual Depression Score. A depression score that falls
outside the stress window should be examined to see
whether learned helplessness is the cause. Ask yourself
these questions:

1. Did my perceived control fall within the stress window?

2. In general do I feel helpless? Do events control me?
   Do I feel trapped?

If the answer to any of these questions is yes, learned helplessness might well be the reason. You can refer to chapter
4 for some general strategies to deal with learned helplessness. I would also recommend that you see your physician
and tell him or her of your symptoms. Disease or purely

physical reasons should be safely put to rest before beginning to work your way out of depression. If during the process of your physical examination you are offered antidepressants, think twice about taking them. Ask your physician whether they are absolutely necessary. It would be better to control your own depression than to give up more sense of control by relying on drugs.

If all three of your scores fall outside the stress window, I would recommend that you immediately select a relaxation skill that is acceptable to you—something that works—and practice, practice, practice. Try the progressive muscle exercise in chapter 5. It works for a large number of people even after the first try. At least try it twice a day for ten days. If all three of your scores fall outside the stress window, then it is absolutely necessary that you see your physician to rule out physical health problems.

BECOMING AWARE OF GOOD STRESS

If all of your scores fall within the stress window, good! You will then be able to learn to use your stress energy even more effectively. Part of the process of using good or adaptive stress for success is to become aware of it first. Try keeping a daily journal to record the times when you were absolutely brilliant and energetic. I prefer this "good news" type of journal over the somewhat heavy task of recording excessive tension stress and failure. A very small notebook that can be carried in a shirt pocket would be just fine. When you feel good or do a good job, write it down along with the time of day, date, task involved, and circumstances. It will take you less than ten minutes a day to do this. How surprised you will be after the first week and then the first month to see what you can learn about your own optimal performance. You will tend to focus on your successes and learn more about what makes you successful. Your stress energy can then be directed toward more success. You will help give anxiety a back seat in your life, rather than the driver's seat. If journal-keeping is impossible for you, try identifying just one activity or job and create an "awareness" week around that single activity. Focus your attention on what, where, when, and how you function in that one situation.

STRESS-WINDOW CHECKLIST

Do you use your stress to accomplish your goals or do you allow it to be channeled into tension stress and anxiety? The checklist that follows contains the common symptoms of anxiety on one side and the signs of good stress or stress-window functioning on the other. Place a check on either the anxiety or stress-window side of the line according to your perception of which most often and most accurately describes your overall experience.

STRESS-WINDOW CHECKLIST

ANXIETY		STRESS WINDOW
1. Vague fears about future	1 2 3 4 5 6 7	Secure over future
2. Feelings of insecurity	1 2 3 4 5 6 7	Feel secure in ability
3. Low energy, fatigue	1 2 3 4 5 6 7	Energetic
4. Sleep problems, awaken tired	1 2 3 4 5 6 7	No sleep problems, awaken rested
5. Depression	1 2 3 4 5 6 7	Not often depressed
6. Feelings of inferiority	1 2 3 4 5 6 7	Feelings of competence
7. Indecisiveness	1 2 3 4 5 6 7	Able to make decisions effectively
8. Intolerance of others	1 2 3 4 5 6 7	Tolerant

9. Feelings of poor health	1 2 3 4 5 6 7	Feelings of being well
10. Loss of interest in activities	1 2 3 4 5 6 7	High level of interest
11. Loss of motivation	1 2 3 4 5 6 7	Highly motivated
12. Inability to focus attention	1 2 3 4 5 6 7	Able to focus attention on task at hand
13. Physical signs perceived as worrisome (heart rate, pulse, aches and pains, light-headedness, fatigue, feelings in stomach, etc.)	1 2 3 4 5 6 7	Physical activation signs perceived as normal
14. Feelings of helplessness	1 2 3 4 5 6 7	Feelings of being in control and effectiveness

A score less than 4 indicates tension-stress functioning. You can compute a *general stress-window* score by:

$$\frac{\text{sum of scores}}{14} = \frac{}{14} = \underline{}$$

You can see that a score of 4 is borderline between the two areas of anxiety and the stress window. Scores above 4 indicate that you are generally functioning in the area of your stress window. This scale will help you identify problem areas, but more importantly, it will also help you identify some of your stress-energy strengths, which are useful in achieving your goals. Looking at each critical life area— work, home, interpersonal relationships, and recreation— use this scale to help discover whether you are operating through your stress window in each of these specific areas. For example, in the area of work, do you have vague fears about the future of your work or do you feel secure? Are you insecure or secure in your work abilities? Do you have enough energy to do your job? Work through all of the bipolar scales for each life area or activity. This information will help you identify your strengths and weaknesses in specific areas, which will be used later in formulating a stress-window program.

If you have read this far and taken all of the tests up to this point, you should have a pretty fair idea of whether you are operating within your stress window. You also have seen some suggestions on how to deal with excessive tension, anxiety, depression, and boredom. The next chapter will describe some physical and mental skills to convert anxiety into adaptive-stress energy and also to generate stress-window energy to help you successfully attain your goals in life.

7: WAYS TO GENERATE GOOD STRESS

How do you get up in the morning? How do you spend your lunch hour? What do you do when you come home or finish a day's work? This chapter offers some nitty-gritty suggestions to help you function in your stress window—to generate and use stress energy to be more successful. Seemingly routine activities of a typical day are critical determinants of your stress level. Pesky little annoyances can push your tension level sky-high. Getting to work or to an appointment on time is a frustrating experience for many people. Activities that have deadlines and are labeled as important will arouse higher levels of stress. Add a small inconvenience— you are ready to go but cannot find your keys, the car needs gas, or your wallet or purse isn't where you thought it would be—and the search is on. If it is not immediately successful, it can become a "search-and-destroy" or "search-and-be-destroyed" mission. Even if the item is found, your stress level will remain elevated. There is pressure to rush and begin to label other small stressors as being more important than they really are. If you are driving, you drive faster or begin to shout at other drivers. You might talk to yourself in a way that increases your stress: "Why does this always happen to *me?* My whole day is ruined." The neat and calm are transformed into the perspiration-soaked and stringy-haired in minutes. There are simple ways to keep your cool for the moment. Moments add up into weeks and months of healthy physical and psychological changes. One of the most urgent and frequent questions asked by those who want to use their stress energy is, "Where do I start?" Start with the little things.

HOW TO GET UP IN THE MORNING

If you feel a little groggy or "not too swift" in the morning, you are experiencing the natural consequences of a lowered activation level. Muscle coordination and memory will not match your intention. Women with lipstick drawn to their ears and men with free-lance surgery done to their throats and faces while shaving are people who try to do too much too soon in the morning. Coax your nervous system into gentle arousal. The stress generated in the morning is the foundation for the day. Here are some suggestions to help you begin the day with you in control.

1. If you awaken feeling tired, you may need to go to bed earlier. Try an extra hour of sleep during the night. Avoid drinking caffeine-laden drinks four hours before going to bed.

2. Organize all of your clothes, papers, and activities for the following day the night before. Find yourself a large, distinctive bowl or basket to hold your keys, wallet, glasses, cigarettes, matches, money, and list of things to be done the next day. The list will free you from spending energy trying to re-

member important things in the morning. You will avoid that sinking feeling you get when you remember halfway to work that you were supposed to give a friend a ride or perhaps call someone to wake them. The list will also let you sleep more peacefully. You will not have to worry about what has to be done the next day. There are times when it pays to forget about responsibilities, and this is one of them. Sometimes a good night's sleep will provide you with new perspectives and solutions for the next day's problems.

3. Give yourself plenty of time to get to work or to begin work if you are working at home. Being pressed for time is a habit, not an uncontrollable event.

4. Gradually move into activity. Springing out of bed into a cold shower is a shock—an extreme stressor. Rude awakenings can produce too much arousal—too much adrenaline. More energy is generated than is needed to meet the challenges of the day.

5. Eat breakfast. Some neurotransmitters are dependent upon blood levels of precursor substances. Each meal supplies the body with needed building blocks for their manufacture.

6. Restrict coffee intake to approximately two cups or less a day. Substitute decaffeinated coffee for everything over two cups, and drink other caffeine-free beverages.

These are only a few ways to start the day. Think about yourself—your needs and situation—and try to develop other ideas to help glide into a new day with plenty of energy reserves and feelings of control.

LUNCHTIME

If your lunch break consists of rushing to a restaurant, standing in line, gulping down your food, and rushing back to work, you are doing yourself a disservice. You are truly "out to lunch." The lunch period is enough time to break the stress cycle, bring your adrenaline level down, and allow your body to restore some of its energy. If you need to lower stress energy, do it through self-control and not through cocktails. Alcohol is a depressant that will suppress energy needed in the afternoon. After relaxing, increase your stress-energy level and return to work. You will feel better and perhaps even avoid the afternoon "slump."

GOING HOME

I've been on the subways in New York City and the freeways in Los Angeles during the rush hour. I'm not about to suggest that you find a quiet spot and relax. Rather, I would remind you that you cannot control everything. When you get home, lower your stress level by using a relaxation technique. It will only take about twenty minutes. Then if you wish to have a cocktail, go ahead. There is some evidence that one to one and a half ounces of alcohol a day reduces the probability of heart attack. But it is important for you to know that you control your stress level. More than one drink will suppress the stress energy needed to remain active during the evening hours. What is the point in working all day to come home to collapse in a corner or fall asleep watching TV? Those four to six evening hours add up to at least 520 hours or twenty-two days a year, not counting Saturdays and Sundays. Those hours can be meaningful and exciting if you operate through your stress window. Some energy-generating techniques to help you raise your stress-energy level after relaxation in the evening will be given later in this chapter.

HOW TO TALK TO YOURSELF

You may think that you do not talk to yourself. Perhaps you do not—out loud, anyway. But most of us talk to ourselves in our minds. The way you talk to yourself can tell you a great deal about yourself. Self-talk reflects your mental sets, that is, the relatively stable ways you perceive yourself and the world.

Albert Ellis, founder of Rational Emotive Therapy, has described several irrational ideas that occasionally guide our thinking. They are the irrational "shoulds," "oughts," and "musts" that creep into our belief systems. Many of these irrational ideas center around perceived helplessness or no-control-sets. I have adapted some of these ideas. Read them and see if any belong to you.

1. Everyone who is important to you must approve of everything you do.

2. You must prove yourself by doing something really important.

3. When things don't go your way, life is terrible.

4. You have little control over your feelings. They are controlled by outside forces.

5. It is easier to avoid unpleasant tasks or events rather than to discipline yourself to face them.

6. The past is more important than the present or future. You are a prisoner of your past.

7. Happiness is achieved by being passive and inactive.

8. Your goodness as a person depends upon successful performance.

9. If you do not find quick solutions to problems, it is terrible.

10. There are many dangerous things in the world. You should worry about them.

I once shared an office with a colleague who talked to himself out loud. He would say things like: "Damn, you fool. You've done it again. What a jerk. Why can't you do anything right?" Once when I dropped a set of papers, he said, "I'm sorry." He was one of those people who took the blame for anything that happened. He knew that it had to be his fault. His self-image devastated his ability to perform well. His sense of control and mastery was near zero.

The next time you talk to yourself, listen to what you are saying. If it is negative, stop it. Substitute positive statements that are rooted in reality. Highlight your successes, not your failures. It is healthier to inventory successes. It makes more sense to see why you succeed rather than emphasize the autopsies of failure. What you think controls your body's stress response as effectively as any outside stressor. If you allow yourself to make statements of noncontrol, then you can expect to feel frustrated, angry, and helpless. You can expect to produce more stress energy than you need. You can expect, in the long run, poor performance and health.

When stress is the topic, tension control is usually the focus of conversation. Controlling excessive tension is only half of learning how to function through your stress window. Generating enough energy is the other half. It is necessary to produce enough energy to meet situational and personal demands. The physical basis for creating energy, as discussed in chapter 3, comes from increasing the arousal level of the nervous system. Specialized physical and mental exercises activate the nervous system to produce stress energy.

PHYSICAL ENERGY-GENERATING TECHNIQUES

RAPID ENERGY EXERCISE

The progressive muscle exercise for relaxation described in chapter 5 can be modified to raise your stress level. Rather than slowly tensing and relaxing different muscle groups of the body, execute rapid alternating contractions. You must activate as many nerve cells as possible to increase the flow of neural information to the central nervous system. It in turn will prepare more muscle fibers to react, which will again raise the level of the activity of the nervous system. This is an activation cycle. Here are the basic steps for the exercise:

1. Loosen tight clothing.

2. Leave eyes open and actively scan your surroundings.

3. Breathe deeply.

4. Rapidly tense one muscle group and release the tension immediately. Repeat each exercise twice.

5. Work through the muscles of the toes, legs, thighs, stomach, back, shoulders, fingers, hands, arms, neck, face, and eyes.

6. For the toes, legs, shoulders, fingers, hands, and arms: contract the left side quickly; release and contract the right side. For example, the sequence for the hands would be left hand contract, release; right hand contract, and release.

Do these contractions as rapidly as possible. By the time you have worked through all of the muscle groups, your activation level will have increased greatly.

ENERGY CALISTHENICS

Any physical exercise that is pleasant for you will raise your activation level. When you use exercise to create energy, the object is not to build muscles or condition the cardiovascular system. That requires an expenditure of bodily resources. The object is to activate the many sensory fibers buried in muscles, skin, and joints. This increases the activity of the brain and in turn increases energy. Do not, therefore, exercise to the point of fatigue. Stop when you begin to feel more activated and alert. Three to ten minutes should be enough time to achieve activation without fatigue.

ENERGY PATTING

This is a stimulating exercise. It will make you feel tingly all over as well as raise your energy level

1. Hold your left hand about three inches over your right hand and begin slapping or patting with your left hand as fast as you can. Regulate the strength of your patting so that it is stimulating but not painful. Rapidly pat all the way up to your right shoulder. Pat each spot on your arm about ten times. Move a hand's width up your arm until you reach your shoulder.

2. Continue up the side of your neck, working around the back of your neck and then to your entire face. Work back down your right side and right leg.

3. Repeat the entire process using your right hand. It is helpful to count rapidly to ten for each area patted until you learn the routine. Incidentally, this is one of those exercises that needs to be performed in pri-

vate lest the uninformed think that you have slipped over the edge of your sanity. The entire exercise takes less than five minutes.

STRETCHING EXERCISES

In their book, *Wrinkles,* Lida Livingston and Constance Schrader (1978) describe several stretching exercises, including some wake-up exercises that are done in bed. Any slow stretching exercise will bring your nervous system into greater activity and increase your energy level. Muscles and joints are richly endowed with movement receptors that alert the brain to produce more energy and prepare the muscles to react.

PHYSICAL EXERCISE

Physical exercise has many faces, some good and some bad. Body build, general physical condition, diet, and personality influence your need for exercise. Everyone needs *regular* exercise. "Regular" means every day if possible and certainly not less than every other day.

Over the years, I have collected some comments about exercise from people in my lectures and seminars.

It's a fad. All of the attention to exercise is a fad that draws the usual fanatic elements of our society. It will pass. I will not be sucked into making a fool of myself.

It's dangerous. Did you read about the jogger who dropped dead of a heart attack while jogging? Runners are always getting hit by cars.

It's expensive. You have to buy expensive equipment to exercise. Medical bills from exercise injuries are costly. Time is money, and it takes time to exercise. I don't have the time.

An elaborate exercise program is necessary. People who do not plan and carry through elaborate and time-consuming exercise programs are fools. They are killing themselves by inactivity.

Nonexercisers are jealous of the self-discipline of regular exercisers. They lack the will power to carry through on an exercise program.

There is a large measure of irrationality and a dash of fact in each of these statements.

WHAT WE KNOW FOR SURE ABOUT EXERCISE

Regular physical exercise regulates the balance of neurotransmitters. Energy level, mood, and motivation are partially dependent upon these transmitters. Regular exercise, for example, has been found to restore the concentration of noradrenaline, one neurotransmitter. People with noradrenaline deficits exhibit depression, lack of motivation, learned helplessness, and sometimes severe mental disorders. Exercise reduces feelings of depression in many cases.

A study of Harvard alumni shows that regular exercise may reduce the risk of heart attack by as much as 35 percent. This study gives a clue as to how much exercise is necessary. There is meaningful reduction of heart attacks with exercise that burns up approximately 2,000 to 2,999 calories per week. More exercise might be beneficial to other bodily systems, but heart attack rate does not seem to be reduced any further. This is a group statistic. Some people may need to exercise a little more and some a little less. Four hours of strenuous activity spread over a week will consume the critical number of calories. The exercise can be jogging, weight lifting, tennis, calisthenics, or any other activity that is physically exerting. One of the effects of this type of exercise is thought to be an increase in high-density lipoproteins, which remove cholesterol deposits from the arteries. Another effect is improvement of lung capacity and circulation. These exercises are called *aerobic* for that reason. Those who exercise regularly report increased feelings of self-esteem, self-confidence, and a more positive body image.

THE REALITY OF EXERCISE: WHAT TO DO AND HOW MUCH

You should exercise about four hours per week according to a regular schedule. Twenty minutes per day of strenuous exercise that works up a sweat will improve your chance for better health and survival. The type of exercise doesn't really matter as long as it involves large movements of muscle groups. Calisthenics, running, bicycling, lifting light weights for endurance, or sports such as tennis are all good.

If you have not exercised regularly for some time, it would be wise to have a physical checkup and to ease into your routine. *Twenty minutes a day*—there is not one legitimate excuse why you cannot take that time to make yourself feel better.

ENERGY-GENERATING TECHNIQUES (MENTAL)

Clearly, your thoughts affect your stress energy. Mental imagery techniques are used in stress reduction. As outlined in chapter 5, thinking of a relaxing scene—imagining it as vividly as possible—produces relaxation. The exercises that follow will use the imagination to create energy. Before using energy-producing exercises, be sure to have rationally accepted that the task must be done. Put ideas of not wanting to do the thing out of your mind. Then, generate the energy needed to attain your objectives. Objectives can be almost anything: going to work, writing a report, cleaning the house, visiting a relative, having sex, going out to dinner —you name it. You will know when you will need to create more energy. You may feel drowsy, weak, or disinterested.

Here is a tip for thinking about something that must be done. The more you actively think about doing something, the greater the probability that you will do it. The problem is that there is a tendency *not* to think about what has to be done when motivation and energy are low. Energy is often diverted to feelings of dreading the task or to worry. Rationalizations flow easily—you are too tired; it isn't important; or you probably couldn't do it anyway. Replace those negative ideas with positive ones, beginning with the rational decision, "I am going to do this."

SELF-CONFIDENCE

Self-confidence is what someone else tells you to have when you don't have it. Self-confidence, like everything else, is a learned attitude. You must practice having ideas of self-confidence. Take a piece of paper and list all of the reasons why you should be confident. This may be a little difficult because of the tendency to focus on failure. This list will give you a set of realistic positive ideas. Use statements from this list to substitute for negative or irrational ideas of helplessness. When a negative self-statement comes into mind, replace it with one of the reasons why you should be self-confident. Try this for a week or two. You will find a decrease in the number of negative self-statements and begin to feel better about your ability to succeed.

BASIC IMAGERY AND FANTASY SKILLS

Using imagination to increase or decrease stress energy is something that you do every day. You may not be aware of how you are doing it, but you are aware of the results. If you use your imagination to think of something erotic, you will find that your energy level begins to increase. If you think of something humorous, you may begin to laugh. As you begin to think of an event, person, or object, you can picture it in your mind. This picturing or image formation is helpful in mentally recreating energy-producing past experiences. It is known that the process of imagery produces physical and mental states that have been associated with actual events. You can harness this skill to create energy with just a little practice. Here are some basic steps for using imagery.

1. Find a relatively quiet and nondistracting environment. As you become more effective, after a week or two, you can begin using imagery skills anywhere to relax or generate energy.

2. On small index cards, write descriptions of at least three scenes that are relaxing and three that are exciting. Try to keep the descriptions as brief as possible.

3. Achieve relaxation by sitting quietly in a chair or using a relaxation technique. Rate yourself on a scale of 0 for the most relaxed that you have ever been to 100 for the most excited that you have ever been. Read the first relaxing scene. Try to picture it. Imagine as many of the sensations associated with the scene as you can. Work through each of the relaxation-scene cards. When you have finished, rate yourself again. This part of using imagery will not have to be repeated once you have acquired some skill in altering your stress level unless you wish to reduce tension stress.

4. Now try reading one of the energy-producing scenes. Again create the sensations that accompanied your experience in that situation. Work through each of the cards, evaluating your activation level using the scale of 0 to 100. The amount of

time spent visualizing each scene and the number of scenes can be varied to produce different amounts of energy.

5. End the practice session by relaxing if you do not have an outlet for the energy you have generated.

6. Practice this procedure or your own variation of it every day for about two weeks. If you wish, keep a record of your self-scaling. It will show you how much control you have gained over relaxing and generating energy.

When you begin practicing imagery skills, you might feel a bit awkward. But let me remind you that you will not be doing something strange or new. You will simply be controlling an important part of your mental life that is often taken for granted. You can gain an awareness of how much fantasy or imagery influences your life by watching for it during the day. Daydreams, for example, are heavily dependent upon imagery. Try keeping a journal for one week. Record the subjects of your fantasies. Although they are only part of your total mental imagery, you will be surprised at their frequency. Many people use mental pictures to solve problems. They visualize how a thing works or how to function in situations. If you still are a skeptic, ask yourself this question: "Is there any person who makes me feel tense when I meet him (her)?" Think of that person *now*. Visualize the face. I would guess that you are experiencing an increase in stress.

ENERGY-SETS
Mental-sets are part imagery and part thought. What you think partially determines how you visualize things in your mind and vice versa. The feeling of looking better after the first day of a diet or exercise program is an example. Nothing has happened to your physical appearance. You look

the same but feel better. Because you feel better, you create a different physical image of yourself. You generate positive ideas about yourself. It is these positive thoughts that produce your improved image and your feeling of well-being. Exercise and dieting take a little longer to produce such results. You create your own realities. You may need to develop some positive sets to replace those negative ones; then you can use your energy to *accomplish,* not worry.

Here are some common mental-sets that help generate good stress. Read them and see which ones you can accept into your self-thinking and self-talk.

Basic survival. I've done all right up to now. There is no reason why I won't succeed in the future. There is no real reason to worry about the future.

Control. I generally control my life. Sometimes things happen that I can't control, but I have been able to adapt to that. In the long run, I control my own destiny.

Personal value. I am a unique person. I am irreplaceable. Basically I have good intentions and I am a good person.

Personal power. I have the potential for achieving anything that I really want. I may have to learn new skills, but I can do that.

Change. Change is good. I can change if I wish. I am not a victim of heredity or my past.

Health. Physical and mental health is dependent to a large degree upon personal habits and the way I think. If I think positively, I will feel better.

Success. Success most often comes from effort. I have the energy within me to achieve success. I can learn to solve most problems.

People. People are basically good. They are all different. They have learned different ideas and skills. They have different fears and hopes. There is no reason to try to control or fear others.

Negative thoughts. Negative thoughts are under my control. They use energy. I can keep them out of my mind and use that energy to achieve my goals.

Failure. Failure is a natural part of life. If I have not been successful in the past, that does not mean that I will not succeed in the future. I can learn from my failures. That knowledge will increase my chances for success.

If you did not find some ideas in that list that apply to your reality, create some for yourself. Write. them down. Rehearse them so that you can substitute them for any negative thoughts. Positive sets will generate good stress. That will increase the probability for success. Success will reinforce your positive thinking.

MEASURING SELF-PERCEPTION

The Q-sort is a method to study self-perceptions. It was developed by psychologist William Stepheson and used by the founder of the Client Centered Therapy, Carl Rogers, and his group. Work through the adjective checklist that follows. First check the adjectives that apply to you—the way you see yourself now. Then check the adjectives with which you would like to describe yourself. If the majority of adjectives are positive, good. Review your strengths. If the traits checked are positive and your two lists are in close agreement, again that's good. That means that the way you perceive yourself agrees with what you want to be. Positive adjectives can be used to develop positive sets. If you wish, put each adjective onto a separate card. You can sort the cards periodically to check your self-image. That is one way to keep positive-energy sets working for you.

SELF DESCRIPTION CHECK LIST

Me	Ideal Me	Me	Ideal Me
	able		irritable
	aggressive		kind
	anxious		lazy
	annoying		lively
	bitter		loving
	caring		mature
	confident		nervous
	cranky		open-minded
	creative		organized
	critical		patient
	cynical		perceptive
	demanding		perfectionistic
	dependable		relaxed
	depressed		resentful
	disciplined		satisfied
	energetic		self-accepting
	fair		self-conscious
	fearful		selfish
	friendly		sensitive
	guilty		shy
	happy		stubborn
	helpless		thoughtful
	inconsiderate		trusting
	independent		uncertain

Work through the list twice. First check the adjectives that describe you now. Second, check the adjectives that describe your ideal self, the ones you would like to apply to you.

SETTING TARGET DATES

Another way to increase your stress energy is to set target dates for important objectives. You will notice that I did not use the word *deadline*. *Target date* is less threatening. It implies that you will aim for it, but might miss the bull's-eye. The fact that you are aiming will increase your stress-energy level. The optimal result would be to set your objectives and target dates in a way that produces stress-window energy. This will take some practice.

There are two potential problem areas in setting target dates. One is to state meaningful objectives. The second is to set realistic time periods to achieve them. A meaningful objective is a specific goal stated in terms of the behaviors and resources required to attain it. Once you know exactly what has to be done, you can make better time estimates.

One thing to remember is that there are things that can happen to cause you to miss a target date. Although you can cushion your time estimates to compensate for little snags, it is impossible to anticipate the unknown, and worry over the unknown is a waste of energy. If an unexpected event deters you from achieving the objective, accept that as a factor over which you have little or no control. Restructure your objectives and target dates. Setting realistic objectives and target dates will enhance your feelings of self-confidence and control. You will be more effective in orchestrating your energy resources and energy demands.

VITAMINS AND ENERGY

Vitamins are often equated with energy. The recommended daily allowance set by the Food and Drug Administration is a guideline and not a hard-and-fast rule. Different constitutions, physical condition, stressors, and activity levels cause considerable variation in bodily demands for vitamins and minerals that are required to help the body produce energy. They are necessary for life and good health.

Do not assume that you are receiving all of the vitamins and minerals necessary from your daily food intake. The current emphasis upon the slim body image, whether it is good for you or not, has millions of people partially starving themselves or eating unbalanced meals.

Even if you think you are preparing well-balanced meals, you might have vitamin deficiencies. Cooking and preserving deplete the vitamin content of most foods. Those vitamins that are finally ingested are only partially absorbed. If you decide, as millions of others do, to take a multivitamin tablet daily just for luck, remember that extrastrength, bio-thrill, supervitamin brand X contains the same kind of vitamin A, C, D, and B as dull, old vitamin brand Z. The difference is that you can buy vitamin Z at one tenth of the cost of X. Taking a multivitamin capsule a day won't hurt. Your body will discard what it doesn't need. If, however, you get into vitamins and start taking megadoses, watch out. Here are some of the disorders caused by excessive dosages of three important vitamins. (Vitamin overdose is called *hypervitaminosis.*)

Vitamin A. headache, vomiting, peeling of the skin, drowsiness, and irritability

Vitamin D. loss of appetite, nausea, vomiting, nervousness, and kidney malfunction or damage

Vitamin K. anemia

Mineral overdose is also possible. I mention these overdose problems to support a recommendation. Do not use self-help books to concoct a megavitamin formula for yourself. If your physical energy levels are low, try taking one multivitamin capsule a day. For anything over that, *see your physician.* Let him or her prescribe a safe vitamin program for you

What you get out of work, play, friendship, sex, and your family is dependent upon how much energy you can generate and invest in these important aspects of your life. The next chapter will discuss some ways to use your stress energy in these life areas. The goal will be to turn anxiety into energy and use it for success.

8: SEX AND STRESS

Sexual activity is stressful. You cannot have sex without stress. But you can have sex without tension. Ideally the stress energy generated before and during sexual activity is labeled as pleasant, but sometimes it is perceived as being unpleasant and tension producing. All of this, of course, depends upon your mental-sets, expectancies, and hormones. Your expectations and physical demands of the situation interact in calling you into action. Just as there is an optimal energy level for work or play, there is an optimal level of stress energy for sex. Barring hormonal influences, most of your sexual behaviors are learned. It has taken you a lifetime to acquire your sexual attitudes and behaviors. If you are not happy with your sex life, do not expect ten easy steps to happiness and success. It will take some thinking, some planning, and some learning.

THE BASIC SEXUAL RESPONSE

Before going on with a discussion of stress and sex, I'd like to review some basic information about the human sexual response. This is only a partial sketch of the physical nature of the human sexual response, important to understanding how stress and sex are related.

The human sexual response is controlled by both the voluntary and involuntary nervous systems. Some of your responses are reflexive and beyond your direct control and others are voluntarily controlled. Parts of the central nervous system involved in the highest forms of human activity such as thinking and imagination also control part of your sexual response. Other aspects of your sexual functioning are controlled by the autonomic nervous system. That is the same nervous system so very important to the body's stress response. The sympathetic branch of that nervous system prepares the body for emergencies. The parasympathetic branch, on the other hand, helps conserve energy during relaxation.

Both the sympathetic and parasympathetic nervous branches of the autonomic nervous system control different parts of the sexual response. This dual innervation has long been known, but its significance for the understanding of sexual problems has only recently been appreciated largely through the work of Masters and Johnson.

THE MALE SEXUAL RESPONSE

The two phases of the male sexual response are erection (vasocongestion) and orgasm. It is rare for a male to have direct voluntary control over erection. He can indirectly control this response through genital stimulation, erotic sensory stimulation, or fantasy. Certain types of physical stimulation or fantasy might also interrupt or prevent erection.

Emission, the first part of orgasm, can voluntarily be delayed. Emission is the contractions of the internal organs which deliver the spermatozoa and seminal fluid. Once emission takes place, ejaculation follows. Males typically enter a refractory period following ejaculation which inhibits further orgasms within a given period of time. This period naturally varies from male to male.

THE FEMALE SEXUAL RESPONSE

Female and male sexual responses are similar. The female's response is biphasic, having a vasocongestive and an orgasmic phase. During the vasocongestive phase, the vagina expands, forms a platform to accommodate the penis, and produces lubrication. The second phase, orgasm, is produced by rhythmical muscle contractions which send sensory information to the brain. One outstanding difference between male and female sexual responses is that, if she wishes, the female may experience multiple orgasms. The refractory period found in the male is absent in females.

SEXUAL PROBLEMS

The human sexual response is best described as a complicated but marvelously integrated sequence of psychological and physical events. Current stress level, hormone secretions, past experience, mental sets, physical condition, and emotional states are but a few of the important influences on sexual behavior. People sometimes think they have problems when in fact they do not. In these cases, information is an effective cure. Sexual problems might be physically caused. There is, for example, evidence that some erectile dysfunctions in males can be related to hormonal imbalances. Some sexual dysfunctions, however, are rooted in excessive tension. Anxiety, depression, feelings of helplessness, boredom, and fatigue are powerful influences on sexual performance. It is clear that some sexual dysfunctions are related to phase 1, vasocongestion and arousal, and are more under the control of the parasympathetic branch of the autonomic nervous system—the part of the nervous system that is so important for relaxation. Primary and secondary erectile dysfunctions in the male are examples of phase 1 problems. A primary erectile dysfunction is a long-term inability to maintain an erection. The secondary erectile dysfunction is temporary. The corresponding problems for females fall under the heading of general sexual dysfunctions and include an inhibition of general sexual arousal and vasocongestive responses. Other dysfunctions involving orgasm for both females and males are associated with the second major phase of the sexual response, generally considered to be related to the energy-producing functions of the sympathetic nervous system.

I have already discussed how these autonomic nervous system responses can become conditioned to various stimuli in the cases of relaxation and tension. You also know that you can learn to gain control over them to increase stress energy or to produce relaxation. Similarly, you can learn to change some aspects of your sexual behavior. If you are experiencing problems, before you begin to worry about your sex life you should rule out physical causes such as hormonal imbalance and disease by making an appointment with your physician. Chronic sexual problems are best left to qualified professionals. Your physician or mental health clinic can recommend a qualified sex therapist if you desire professional help. You should also realize that some apparent sexual problems occur now and then as natural consequences of the tension of living. An occasional problem does not mean that you have a sexual dysfunction.

SEX MYTHS

Current macho hype and popular distortion of human sexuality would have us feel insecure about anything less than ecstasy. If you were keeping a score card of your sexual experiences, it would be an exceptional record indeed that showed 100 percent optimal performance and satisfaction. Some males, for example, are horrified to find that they might lose an erection during lovemaking, but yet, that is normal. It can be regained. This can be explained by the natural increases and decreases in nervous system activity underlying physiological arousal. Some people are disappointed if they do not achieve orgasm, but there will be another time. Tune out the barrage of absurd sexual myths and tune in to your own feelings and body.

Here are just ten of seemingly countless irrational and false ideas about sex that generate excessive anxiety. These are the top ten that I have collected during therapy sessions over the last few years.

1. Sex is bad. You should not enjoy it.

2. If a woman does not experience orgasm, she will not enjoy the sexual encounter.

3. A male should never lose an erection during lovemaking.

4. Sex is a duty to be performed on demand.

5. Women ought to assume passive roles in sexual activity and should not be assertive.

6. For a male, his performance is what should be important during lovemaking.

7. Mutual orgasm is necessary for good sex.

8. If either partner does not seem to enjoy a sexual encounter as much as usual, it signifies boredom, a loss of love, or rejection.

9. Declines or increases in sexual activity are abnormal.

10.   Couples shouldn't talk about what stimulates and satisfies them sexually.

These situations and ideas can create enough anxiety to disrupt the delicate nervous system and hormonal processes that regulate sexual activity. Sensitive communication with your partner can go a long way to reduce anxiety flowing from the guilt, anger, and disappointment that often result from these irrational ideas.

WHAT YOU DON'T KNOW HURTS YOU, OR I DON'T WANT TO TALK ABOUT IT

You probably hear or read something about sex almost every day. Although there is an abundance of talk, there is little meaningful communication. Many talk about sex with their friends, but do not communicate with spouses or lovers. An open and sensitive exploration of each other's sexual feelings will go a long way in taking some of the anxiety out of sex. In addition, I strongly recommend that everyone at some time read a rational account of sexual functioning. You don't have to be an expert, but it is helpful to know about basic sexual anatomy and functioning. That knowledge can help reduce sexual anxiety and also enhance your sexual experience. Here, for example, are a few observations that might help take some of the anxiety out of sex.

1. Older men and women need more stimulation during sexual activity.

2. Younger women need more sensitivity and stimulation from their partners.

3. It is natural for older men (fifty and over) to require more stimulation to maintain arousal.

4. Clitoral stimulation is important to the female's feelings of pleasure and attainment of orgasm.

5. Communication about personal feelings and sexual sensitivities between partners will help avoid the formation of irrational ideas.

Three points emerge from these facts: (1) As we age our sexual functioning changes—generally we require more stimulation; (2) sexual differences between men and women require different levels of stimulation; and (3) communication between partners can help reduce tension. The following case is a typical example of how excessive tension and anxiety can influence our sex life. You will note how sexual disappointments spill over into other areas of life.

An attractive woman, in her early forties, explained that her husband was no longer sexually interested in her. Unfortunately she felt that it was her fault. She tried to improve her appearance and to please him by working harder. She said that they had sex only about once a month, and that was not very satisfactory. When she tried to discuss the matter, her husband became angry and said that he did not want to talk about it. He was being considered for promotion at work and was making an all-out effort by taking on extra work and working extra hours. He wasn't sleeping well, felt depressed, and was obviously very tense. His decline in sexual activity was a natural response to the chronic excessive tension and anxiety that he was experiencing. The problem was not with his wife or that he did not care for her, but that he was not coping with his own tension. He was tense about his sexual decline. He also interpreted his wife's attempts to discuss it and her extra efforts as additional pressures or demands on him. Excessive tension, a lack of understanding of how tension affects sex, and a lack of communication contributed to this couple's crisis.

It is a simple matter to say that either too little or too much stress energy causes sexual problems. Sex like stress is a complex response—dependent upon your physiology as well as your thoughts. Sexual activity is necessary, natural, and normal, but many of the ideas concerning sex in our culture are maladaptive. Irrational prohibitions and expectations run head on into a strong physiological need for sexual activity. As that need builds, complex and powerful nervous system and hormonal changes occur in the body, and when the need is met, more changes occur. Remembering that stress and sex share the same bodily resources makes it easier to understand why excessive tension that builds through the day, for example, spills over into the sexual response. If tension or anxiety is brief, sexual drive and activity might increase. But chronic anxiety eventually leads to a reduction in sexual activity.

THE NEED FOR STIMULATION: VARIETY IS THE SPICE OF LIFE

The human nervous system responds to change. Novelty raises the energy level of the nervous system. Repetitions of the same sensory stimulus cause a decrease in nervous system activity. This is called *habituation.* Habituation most certainly is involved whenever you "get used to" some stimulus in your environment. You can rehabilitate a habituated stimulus by assigning it a special place in your thoughts—by making it psychologically important. When it comes to sex, psychological habituation is not uncommon. Periodic apparent boredom or disinterest is a frequent occurrence. Boredom or lack of interest left unattended might result in a chronic decline of sexual activity or enjoyment. Sex becomes another chore. Perhaps even something to get out of the way quickly so that you can go to sleep. This is the "honeymoon is over" syndrome. Anxiety is a consequence of sexual boredom. Frequently this additional anxiety is converted into hostility and anger.

How do you revive a dying love life? One solution, and one that might not be an attractive alternative, is to choose a variety of sexual partners. Novelty in sexual partners seems to have an invigorating effect on sexual activity. This is referred to as the "Coolidge effect" by many behavioral scientists. President Coolidge's wife, legend has it, commented that barnyard males seem to possess excessive sexual prowess. President Coolidge supposedly replied that yes, they did, but he also noted that they were involved with a variety of partners. Sexual experimentation for both sexes is a fact in our society. As a psychologist I cannot recommend this as a solution to married or unmarried couples. I have spent countless hours with couples who were having serious difficulties in attempting to cope with outside sexual relationships. It is possible that I have only seen those who obviously were having trouble and that many people are happily revitalizing their sex life through variety. It is important to realize that the ability to survive in this complex world of ours is strongly dependent upon the maintenance of intimate social relationships. Those relationships are often sexually sensitive. Even when both people involved in them say that they both accept the idea of sexual freedom, guilt and anxiety are all too common.

SEXUAL RUTS

Just how much of a sexual rut can one get into? Well, a friend of mine once told me that she ate an apple while having sex with her husband. I couldn't resist asking her why. She said that she was hungry. If you feel like reading a book or eating an apple during sex, it could be that you are in a sexual rut. You are uninterested. Remembering that your nervous system responds to novelty and change, an obvious solution to sexual boredom is to vary time, place, and activity. The key to getting out of a sexual rut is communication. Everyone talks about what to have for dinner or where to go out to eat, but when it comes to sex, nothing is said. Minor sexual surprises can add some zest, but before you start wearing exotic costumes and dragging out the whips, first talk it over with your partner.

PRACTICE DOESN'T MAKE PERFECT

Popular literature and films reinforce the notion of the perfect lover. Both partners in a sexual encounter are supposed to give and experience pleasure perfectly. In the extreme it has been suggested that the male should be capable of marathon sexual performance, perhaps satisfying countless women. Women, on the other hand, are expected to experience dynamic orgasms even during the most hurried encounters. If they don't, by the way, they are expected to fake them. These are irrational ideas that ruin spontaneity and mutual satisfaction. They often provoke attempts to overcontrol sexual performance. Worrying about performance increases anxiety and detracts from experience. Anxiety has the effect of increasing the stress-energy level of the body. When one partner is considerably more anxious or physiologically aroused than the other, problems can occur. It is helpful if both partners start out at the same relative level of stress energy. This is called *energy-synching*.

ENERGY-SYNCHING
While it might add a little spice to your sex life, being dragged into the boudoir via a sneak attack is not always welcomed. This is particularly true after you have already been dragged through a knothole at work and have established an expectancy of going home to relax quietly. If one partner has too much energy and the other not enough, this can lead to the "I have a headache" or "I am too tired" syndrome. It is during times like that when that old homily, "Pretend you are enjoying it," comes to mind. There are advantages for both partners to start out at roughly the same

level of stress energy. One obvious effect is to help match your mutual sexual phases of vasocongestion and orgasm. One way to do this is to spend some time relaxing together. Lie down together, perhaps massage tired back muscles or just be quiet for about twenty minutes, so that you are both starting from relatively similar arousal levels. From there you can gradually increase your stress-energy levels through mutual sensory stimulation, for example, stroking and touching. Occasionally you might both fall asleep. Don't worry about that. If you schedule a quiet time for every day or at least every other day, there will be plenty of opportunities.

You can, of course, both start at high energy levels too. I often suggest that clients having difficulty controlling tension involve their spouses or partners in their relaxation and exercise programs. I am not sure whether it is the energy-synching, the sharing of a common activity, or the reduction of tension, but many couples report improvements in their sex life.

A FINAL WORD ABOUT SEX

Stress is most assuredly related to sexual arousal. Too much or too little stress energy is correlated with certain types of sexual dysfunctions. Controlling energy levels, energy-synching, might help enhance your sexual experience, but you should keep the complex nature of your sexual response in mind. Hormones, stress, and mental-sets all influence sexual functioning. The attitudes you have developed about your partner and how you communicate with each other are very important. Many sexual problems are rooted deeply in emotions. If you feel that you have a chronic sexual problem, it would be best to seek professional help.

9: STRESS AND RELATIONSHIPS

The only way a relationship among people can be stress-free is if all of the parties are dead. All relationships between people are stressful. What we need to do is to try to maximize good stress in our interactions with others. Even at that, the road will be a little bumpy now and then. Improving your interactions with people is a lifelong process. Everyone is unique in his/her psychological and physical makeup. Each person, then, becomes a unique case for your understanding and effort.

We often try to reduce the uncertainty of interactions with others by forming expectations and making certain decisions about their behavior. Generally these expectations and decisions are based more on emotion than on fact. Prejudice is one outcome of irrational expectations. Prejudice would have a difficult time surviving if human expectations were based more on fact than emotion. The fact is, being emotional is part of being human. We are also rational but our rationality is somehow overemphasized whenever we talk about ourselves. In "The Critic as an Artist," Oscar Wilde says it very nicely: "Man is a rational animal who always loses his temper when he is called upon to act in accordance with the dictates of reason." What we need, then, is a rational habit that we can easily call into action to help us develop more satisfactory relationships with those people who are important to us. Approaches that are based upon telling us specifically *how* to behave in different situations—work, home, or social gatherings—are not very effective, mainly because human behavior is so varied and unpredictable no matter what the situation. We must remain flexible in our relationships. For example, if you wanted to feel more assertive or increase your self-esteem, you would not solve your problem by telling everybody off. You would increase your problems. But interestingly enough, that is the way some people operate. We sometimes develop expectations and emotions about others that are relatively inflexible. They are not based on fact or rational thinking but on gut reaction. Many of our irrational ideas about people are formed early in life, but we are never too old to become irrational. We form new ideas about our relationships throughout all phases of life.

Although we are all different, we do confront similar problems in the different phases of our lives, from childhood to the later years. We try to solve these problems in different environments and with different physical and psychological resources. These, then, are individually unique biosocial problems involving our selves, our environments, and others. Child-rearing, for example, is a popular topic. How do you raise your children? Should you be permissive or strict? The answers to questions such as this are dependent upon the behaviors and feelings of you and your child and the situation. If you are always permissive, your behavior could be regarded as inflexible or not adaptive. How many of us have seen children destroying a house they are visiting while the parents look on with approval. In that case it is called, "allowing your child to express her or himself."

What is really needed to get through life's crises is a systematic decision-making habit, a habit that becomes as automatic as tying your shoes.

The habit I am recommending is a simple decision model that can easily be remembered by its initials, AIMS. I have been describing this model all through this book, but now it is time to put it into a form that can easily be remembered and practiced.

AIMS: A PROGRAM TO USE STRESS ENERGY EFFECTIVELY

1. *A* stands for awareness, awareness of your level of stress, your thoughts, the *facts* of the situation. As well as you possibly can, gather as much information about those with whom you are interacting and the demands of the situation.

2. *I* stands for identification of the problem, which sometimes requires sifting through overly simplified and irrational explanations.

3. *M* refers to management, those behaviors or resources that will be needed to cope with the situation.

4. *S* is self-evaluation. How well did things go? What could you do the next time to make things better?

Chapter 5 describes AIMS in greater detail.

Like all habits, AIMS must be practiced so that you automatically run through these simple basic steps even during heightened emotional states. If you do, you will be able to create more effectively just the right amount of stress energy to meet the demands of most situations.

The objectives for this chapter are to show how AIMS can be used to produce the most adaptive amount of stress energy to aid the development of social relationships throughout life and to identify some of the life crises that occur from childhood to the later years. You can do three things to cope with these crises: adjust, adapt, and compromise.

Adjustment refers to the changes you make in your environment and adaptation to the psychological and physical changes that occur in you. Optimizing these life processes is the theme of this book. Good sense tells you, however, that optimization of stress energy to work through your stress window is a goal requiring a lifetime of striving. To say that everything is going to work out 100 percent of the time is naïve. Compromise is not only possible but necessary for healthy survival. We begin to learn how to adapt, adjust, and compromise during childhood. Those early experiences are mostly centered on our interpersonal relationships. We begin to develop our sense of perceived control and mastery from these relationships. The beginnings of whether you feel generally in control of the major events that shape your life or whether you feel battered by the events and people around you are rooted in your early relationships. You are not a prisoner of those experiences, however. Your coping behaviors are shaped through learning, and what has been learned earlier in life can be and often is replaced by new learning.

CHILDHOOD

Children are not commonly taught a method to solve problems, particularly interpersonal ones. Many adults discriminate against children by assuming a lack of reasoning or problem-solving capacity. I remember being taught that a child does not reach the "age of reason" until the age of seven. Adults are often surprised, irritated, or amused when a child gives evidence of logical thinking. What are we to assume? Is a person a subhuman species to the age of seven, eighteen, or twenty-one years and incapable of rational thinking? I think not. If children do not seem to be able to make decisions that are acceptable to adults, it may be due to inexperience, but there are two other reasons for this:

1. Children are not taught simple, systematic ways to solve problems.
2. Children learn a great deal through modeling. They imitate the behaviors of their parents.

How many parents sit down with their children to teach them a decision-making process like AIMS? Because early interpersonal relationships and healthy environmental mastery experiences are so important for the development of future coping skills, my research team is translating AIMS into programs easily understood by children of different ages. We are also teaching children how to manage stress. It is our belief and experience that children can begin to learn effective coping strategies from the time they learn to speak on up to adolescence. The learning process does not stop there, of course; it continues throughout life. Children can learn what it means to adjust, adapt, and compromise. Rather than being taught that everything will always turn out all right, they learn that in the long run most things turn out all right and that they can be very effective in making sure that they do. The key is that the training must be explicit. The steps of optimizing coping behaviors, such as those in AIMS, have to be taught in ways the child can understand and enjoy.

One way children learn how to cope is through modeling—imitating the behavior of parents, other relatives, and friends. Parents, however, are the most important behavioral models—the molds for their children's behavior. The way parents deal with their own stress in relationships is reflected in the relationships of their children. If a child is acting "childish," it is often because he or she is copying the behavior of the parents. I often find that parents are aware of modeling but in a rather distorted way. A parent may shout or hit a child to get him/her to get ready for school in the morning. The child goes to school and shouts or strikes out at other children. If the teacher requests a parent conference to discuss the problem, some parents respond by saying, "What are you teaching my child in this school? He is not like that at home." Now to be sure, some children do learn those sorts of things at school; but if the parents are serving as caring and rational problem solvers, maladaptive modeling will not stand much of a chance of taking root. Act as you would like your children to act. If you do that and spend time teaching your children how to solve problems, you will help them manage their stress so that it helps them cope with their relationships and environments.

Most of the crises of childhood are interpersonal. They often involve changes in parent-child interaction. Starting school, divorce or separation of parents, parental abuse, death or illness of a parent, death or illness of a brother or sister, and illness that requires hospitalization are some of the interpersonal stressors for children. The family is the first social organization that helps the child cope with stress. Physical or emotional separation from the family can produce severe anxiety in the life of a child.

STARTING SCHOOL

Starting school may seem like a trivial matter to an older person but is a trauma for children. One study (Kellam and Schiff, 1967) showed that first-grade teachers rated 70 per cent of their students as having maladaptive behaviors. I do not think that this should surprise anyone. Children leave their homes and parents to go to a strange environment filled with strangers. If a child does not know what to expect in this new and overstimulating experience, excessive anxiety will produce some worrisome behaviors. Some of these behaviors are aggressiveness, hostility, depression, crying, withdrawal, insomnia, nightmares, loss of appetite, bed-wetting, uncooperativeness, vomiting, timidity, hyperactivity, and increased dependency. These are only a few of the maladaptive behaviors that might arise during the first few weeks of school. Generally these problems will disappear after two or three months, but some will persist and reach serious proportions in 2 to 10 percent of children. One very constructive approach to helping children adapt healthily to entering school is a type of stress-inoculation program that involves preschool meetings of parents, teachers, and children. Parents can come to terms with their own fears about what is going to happen to their children in school. Parents and children together can become aware of their apprehensions and establish mutual support systems to help one another cope with the changes in their life. Many communities sponsor preschool programs. You can call your local school, PTA, or mental health clinic for information.

SEPARATION FROM PARENTS

Unlike the usually temporary stress reactions of going to school, divorce or separation from one or both parents can cause chronic stress problems for children. A 1970 study by Dr. John McDermott, professor and chairman of Psychiatry; University of Hawaii at Honolulu; on the effects of divorce on children shows that if children are given support at home, that is, an opportunity to release emotion and receive extra attention, they are able to cope more effectively. Children lacking a base of support are described as being sad and angry. Their interpersonal relationships abound with anger and grief.

Death of a parent is a serious crisis for children. Children often are not able to comprehend a sense of loss. They can observe the sadness of a surviving parent or relative but may not fully, emotionally understand what has happened. Their reactions range from hyperactivity to depression. The bereavement of a child might spill over into interpersonal relationships as anger, unconcern, depression, or a need for dependence. This is one case where the remaining members of the family can help one another by sharing their grief. Unfortunately, children are all too often sent away to friends or relatives.

CHILD ABUSE

Child abuse and neglect are serious problems in our society. Some of my colleagues and I did some research and wrote a paper to help social service agencies aid abused children and their families. We found that the incidence of child abuse and neglect occurred at a rate of approximately 540 per 100,000 population (Bommer, Goodgion, Pease, and Zmud, 1977), which adds up to over a million cases per year. In writing our paper we reviewed the research on child abuse and found that

1. Child-abusing parents are described as immature, self-centered, having deep-seated hostility, having an impaired ability to show affection, and feeling inadequate or helpless in their role as parents.

2. There is a high correlation between the way people were treated as children and the way they treat their own children.

3. Children who have suffered from abused or neglected childhoods are less likely to experience happy and productive later lives.

Three important statements about stress management and interpersonal relationships may be drawn from these findings. First, parents who have not learned how to keep their own stress under control are often not able to manage the unexpected stresses of parenthood. Some of these stresses will be discussed later in this chapter. Second, abusing parents often have been abused by their own parents.

They, in effect, model the parenting behaviors of their own parents. Third, abused children frequently do not completely recover from these early traumatic experiences. They often feel guilty about their own abuse and somehow feel that they have brought it on themselves. Furthermore, children develop a sense of learned helplessness. Where can they turn? What can they do to prevent abuse? The children are afraid to ask others for help and learn that there is little or nothing that they can do to escape or avoid abuse. They learn that they have little control over the events that influence their life. They develop mental-sets of helplessness that can shape their coping responses for the rest of their life. They, in turn, repeat the cycle with their own children.

PUNISHMENT

I'm not going to tell you within these few paragraphs how to raise your children. No paper, book, or "expert" can do that. What I am going to do is to describe briefly some of what we know for sure about using punishment to change the behaviors of children and how stress figures into this process.

There are two kinds of learning that are very important in the development of human behavior. One type involves the autonomic nervous system, and the kinds of responses learned are those of the smooth muscles of the blood vessels, intestines, and glands. These responses are "forced" or elicited by certain stimuli. Electric shock or pain, for example, elicits a number of responses that are coordinated into a stress response or unpleasant emotion. Other stimuli that are present can also, from that time, elicit the fear or stress response. One pairing of a stimulus with a shock or experience of pain is often all it takes to elicit intense fear or anger to future presentations. When we punish by inflicting physical or emotional pain, we are doing much more than just reducing the probability that a child will repeat the undesirable behavior. We are conditioning emotional responses such as fear and anger to the punishing parent. These responses can last for years.

A second kind of learning, operant conditioning, occurs when a behavior is emitted (not forced by the nature of a stimulus) and then is followed by favorable or unfavorable consequences. These consequences determine the probability of future occurrences of the behavior. Applying positive consequences and removing negative ones (punishment) increase future occurrences. Removing positive consequences and applying negative ones decrease them.

Parents were aware of these rules of behavioral change long before psychologists studied them in the laboratory. But there are some serious pitfalls in this approach, especially concerning the effects of punishment. Punishment may temporarily prevent the occurrences of undesired behavior, even that is dependent upon three conditions: (1) punishment should immediately follow the undesired behavior; (2) punishment should be clearly associated with the undesired behavior; and (3) punishment should be consistent, that is, the undesired behavior should always be punished whenever it occurs. If those conditions are fulfilled, punishment still might not be effective because: (1) its effectiveness is dependent upon the presence or threatened presence of the punishing agent; and (2) what the punishing agent thinks is a punishment is not perceived that way by the one who is being punished. Here is an everyday example of the failure of punishment.

While shopping one day, I observed the most incredible display of Brat and Parental Behavior. A mother was shopping with her child. The child, about four or five years old, was riding in the shopping basket. He screamed, hit, threw things out of the basket, and knocked things off the shelves nonstop for about forty-five minutes. Even when they were temporarily out of sight, I knew where they were by the screaming and crashing sounds. The mother was a torrent of verbalisms, "Don't do that! Do you want to get slapped? Wait until I tell your father! Your father will spank you! Don't scream! Don't touch that! I'm sick of your screaming!" Her screaming and the child's screaming nearly drove the rest of us shoppers, who were already anxious, into organizing a lynch mob. She spanked and slapped the child two or three times, but that didn't have any effect other than making him more angry.

Allow me to speculate about the mechanics of the failure of punishment in this case. First of all, the number of threats of punishment far outnumbered actual punishment by about 20 to 1. (I counted verbalizations and actual punishments for approximately thirty minutes.) If punishment is to be effective, it must be carried out when threatened. Second, the child's monster behavior was receiving an incredible amount of attention from his mother. What the mother thought was punishment was actually a reinforcer. Attention is a strong reinforcer, often stronger than the negative aspects of punishment. Even one of the shoppers contributed to providing attention to the child. She was a very pleasant woman, who spoke to the child in a sympathetic tone, "My, aren't we unhappy today?" He stuck his tongue out at her. Finally, as it almost always does, punishment evoked negative emotions in the one being punished. In this case, anger. Negative emotions often interfere with the acquisition of new behaviors.

Punishment will always produce stress. The trick is to channel that stress into positive consequences. Here are some guidelines for making the use of punishment more effective and the stress that is produced more constructive.

HOW TO PUNISH WHEN YOU MUST

1. The target behavior should be clearly identified and the nature of the punishment clearly described to the child before the first punishment is delivered.

2. Punishment must occur immediately after the undesired behavior.

3. Every occurrence of the undesired response should be punished.

4. An alternative acceptable response should be clearly identified. This will enable the stress energy generated to be channeled into learning a new behavior.

5. The acceptable response should be positively reinforced or rewarded.

If you follow these guidelines, punishment still might produce unpleasant consequences for both you and your child. Punishment (1) increases stress and negative emotions; (2) leads to a tendency to avoid the punishing agent; (3) teaches the one who is being punished how to punish through imitation; and (4) creates tension in the one who is punishing.

Considerable interpersonal stress is generated during punishment. Two conditions can help prevent that stress from becoming maladaptive. The first is to establish a strong base of support for the child in the family by creating an atmosphere of trust and genuine caring. The second is to follow the above guidelines systematically.

Although punishment produces what are at first glance seemingly quick results, positive reinforcement is a more constructive approach for the long run. Positive reinforcement is simple enough. Positive reinforcers or rewards are given after a desired behavior has occurred. This increases the probability of that behavior occurring again. Whenever possible undesired behaviors should be ignored. A detailed discussion of positive reinforcement is beyond the scope of this book, but if you wish to find out more about it, I can recommend *Behavior Modification Principles, Issues and Applications* by Craighead, Kazdin, and Mahoney (Boston: Houghton Mifflin Co., 1976).

The most important principle to remember when you are punishing or reinforcing the behavior of a person.

whether an adult or child, is to relate clearly the rewards or punishments to the person's behavior. If interpersonal stress is to be kept within the realm of the stress window, each of us must learn to perceive that the reinforcements and punishments that we receive from others are directly related to our behaviors. Confusion or ambiguity in the delivery of punishments or rewards induces helplessness, anger, or frustration. Verbalizations of "It doesn't matter what I do, I'll get in trouble for it" and "I don't know what he/she wants. Nothing I do pleases her/him" are examples of mental-sets that produce unhealthy stress and cause unhappy relationships.

ADOLESCENCE

Adolescence is a period of dramatic physical and social change. It is a period of rapid physical growth with all of the accompanying dramatic hormonal changes. The activity level of an adolescent as a rule increases. They seem to have endless energy. They begin to change the nature of their relationships by moving toward intimacy. It is a time of testing mastery in social relationships. A time of testing their independence with parents. A healthy adolescent experiences the joy of mastery and the excitement of change. Change is not perceived as a threat but as an adventure.

This is an important time in life to have acquired a decision-making habit already. Stress energy needs to be guided by the adolescent. It is important for them to be trusted by their parents to make decisions for themselves. AIMS is a rational habit that maximizes information, alternative choices, action, and evaluation. Many poor decisions that are chalked up to immaturity are simply due to a lack of information. Adolescents will more easily tolerate questions concerning the process that they have gone through to arrive at a decision than the content of the decision. You can ask, "Did you gather all of the information, generate several alternatives, and then make your decision?" without questioning the wisdom of the decision. If you criticize the decision or rule it out before understanding the reasoning, you stand a good chance of damaging trust in your relationship. This does not mean, however, that you must be permissive. You can set whatever rules you wish, but they need to be rational and consistently applied.

Trust in human relationships is dependent upon doing what we say we are going to do. If we cannot, it is necessary to explain the reasons for our failure. If you promise punishment and do not carry through, or if you promise reward and do not carry through, your children will learn that punishments and rewards are not related to their behaviors. They will also learn that they cannot trust a very important person in their life. They will also learn that their behaviors are not effective, which often results in anger, frustration, and depression.

EARLY ADULT YEARS

The major interpersonal events of the early adult years are the development of intimacy in forming long-term relationships and becoming responsible for self-support through work, marriage, and parenthood. Each of these developments is a stressor that adds special energy demands to our life.

The stressors of forming long-term intimate relationships such as living together or marriage are related to the development of new roles. There is a sharing of resources, maintenance of living quarters, recreational time, friends, and emotions. The problems of intimate relationships are certainly well documented. Some of the reasons for separation or divorce include: mental cruelty (whatever that is), adultery, nonsupport, chewing with the mouth open, leaving the toilet seat up, burning out the clutch in the family car, and so forth. Rather than dwell on the negative reasons for separation, let's look at the positive aspects of a long-term relationship as an energy resource.

Much of our resiliency and coping power comes from our relationships. When intimate relationships are discussed, sexual activity is often singled out as the critical ingredient. Sex is important, but there is another greater quality of an intimate relationship. A relationship provides a system of resources that can enhance the ability of the participants to adapt healthily to the demands made upon them. It is synergistic. The combined coping or adaptation potential of a relationship is greater than the sum of the individual coping strengths of its participants. That is the full potential of human relationships. Of course, things can go wrong. All of that energy can also become destructive. The probability of that happening increases when the course of the relationship is directed entirely by emotion. Relationships naturally create demands and generate stress, and if they are not managed by the participants, all of that stress may be converted into anxiety. The case that follows will illustrate this point through the life event of parenthood.

LET'S HAVE A BABY

Ann and Roger were married for about two years when they decided to have a baby. They both agreed that they wanted a baby and thought that they could manage it financially. When Ann became pregnant all of the in-laws were pleased. They had been pressuring the couple for grandchildren. The pregnancy was exciting for both of them. Their energy was spent on shopping for clothes, toys, equipment, showers, and selecting a name. The baby was born healthy and was brought home. The happiness of this situation soon evaporated. Both Ann and Roger became very tense. They were plagued with colds and flu. Their interactions were tense and hostile. They both had complaints. Ann complained of having too much to do, a loss of energy, loss of sleep, and feelings of being trapped at home. Roger's complaints were similar: loss of sleep, inability to relax, disruption of activities, more work than expected, a loss of income because Ann had quit her job, and a feeling of being trapped by his new responsibilities. In Ann and Roger's case, a number of difficulties led to excessive tension. They had not accurately assessed the energy requirements of having a baby. They had not developed a plan to meet the potential new demands. They also failed to communicate. Each because of his/her fatigue and increased anxiety thought that the other was being inconsiderate. Each thought that he/she was carrying the bulk of the load. These were irrational ideas that generated more tension. In the end they solved their own difficulties by writing down how they felt, their problems, the resources they had between them, and a plan to cope with the new demands. They also agreed to set aside a period of time during each day to discuss the effectiveness of their program. By following these steps, Ann and Roger were able to organize the resources of their relationship to direct their stress energy into adaptive coping behaviors rather than maladaptive tension. They also strengthened their relationship.

LATER YEARS

There are some special problems associated with aging, but I want to assure you that senility is not one to cause excessive worry. Fewer than 5 percent of people over sixty-five years of age are troubled with senility. Senility is an organic brain syndrome in which there is a deterioration of the brain resulting in emotional and behavioral problems. It usually occurs later in life. Although senility is often used as a source of humor, there is nothing funny about it. It is a serious affliction in those few who have it. There are few changes in the brain and nervous system that cause problems for older people, but those largely involve the senses, for example, vision, hearing, taste, and smell. It was once thought that nerve cells died at an accelerated rate as a function of age, but that does not seem to be true. There is some evidence that the branchings of nerve cells might decline in number, but even that seems to be dependent upon activity and stimulation. If you lead an active life from the age of sixty-five on, the nervous system should continue to grow.

One interesting and sensible theory concerning aging is the Brain Endocrine Theory. The idea of this theory is that there are brain centers that coordinate the major hormones of the body related to growth, sex, and metabolism. There are most probably hereditary factors that control cell replacement and ultimately longevity, but the rate of aging, how fast we age, is also controlled by the brain. Those same brain systems and hormones are involved in our stress responses. It is almost a certainty that stress influences the rate of aging. You have probably seen someone who has been subjected to intense stressors age very rapidly. I think that photographs of some of the presidents of the United States show this effect. Within a relatively short period, they age quickly. As we begin to learn to control our stress response, we may find that we also slow the rate at which we age.

The significant stressors of later life come from changes in work activity, interpersonal relationships, and health. They are all interrelated. Retirement, changes in relationships brought about by poor health or the death of friends, and your own health are powerful stressors. As you might expect, the key to using this stress is through a cognitive habit like AIMS. That will help you efficiently channel stress energy into constructive adaptation. Here are some strategies that will help you cope with some of the changes of later life:

1. If intimate relationships change because of the death of a friend or spouse, establish new relation-

ships. Your ability to cope with stressors is enhanced through the resources of close relationships. They are necessary.

2. As the time for retirement approaches, begin planning for your postretirement life. The best time to start planning is around the age of fifty. That is early enough to organize the resources needed for planned changes in work habits. If you wish to continue working, perhaps a second career will be your choice. Although some colleges still discriminate on the basis of age, training for a new career is almost unlimited. Do not think that you are too old to go back to school. If older people have problems in going back to school, it is not because of "brain power" but because of a lack of planning and organization.

3. Do not be forced into inactivity by the irrational thinking of others. It is natural and necessary for us to keep physically active, make new relationships, engage in sexual activity, and just "plain, old" play.

4. Manage your stress energy. Learn how to relax. Learn how to create energy. When you find yourself losing interest in hobbies, friends, or activities, start scheduling them. The only good reason for cutting back on activities is because of health problems. Listen to your physician. Follow his/her advice, not the advice of friends or others. Remember that you have a need for stimulation. The nervous system thrives on it. Keep active.

5. Manage your diet and maintain a regularly scheduled physical activity program.

COMMUNICATION: DID YOU SAY "YOU DIDN'T HEAR WHAT I SAID"?

There are three major kinds of human behavior involved in communication: verbal communication, nonverbal communication, and listening. The way we communicate can increase or reduce stress in relationships.

Many interpersonal stresses come from contradictory communications between people with close emotional ties, called *double binds.* Suppose you wish to go out with a friend to a film or play and you ask your spouse if that would be all right. Your spouse may develop a hurt look and say something like this: "Okay, go ahead. That's okay with me. I'll just stay home—alone. I'll find something to do. Perhaps I'll just go to bed early." The verbal message is yes. The nonverbal message is no. What are you to do? You are a victim. You cannot comfortably do anything. If you go, you might feel guilty. If you stay home, you might feel angry. Besides that, if you decide to stay home you might get another double-binding message, "Don't stay home because of me. You never go out." Whatever you do your stress level will increase along with emotions.

Emotions are expressed during communication in many ways and are frequently not very constructive. Here are some other pitfalls of communication that generate tension in relationships:

Projective labeling. During emotional states there is a tendency to label others with the emotion that you are experiencing. One's own emotions are projected onto others. For example, if you feel angry there is a tendency to label others as being angry when they are not.

Name-calling. When a person feels hurt or angry, he/she may express his/her emotion by name-calling, for example, you are a turkey, a jerk, mean, insane.

Harsh commands. Feelings of being hurt are often translated into commands such as get out, shut up, leave me alone, go jump in the lake, or forget it.

Judgmental statements. When emotions run high, evaluative statements are common, for example, fair versus unfair, good versus bad, pleasant vs. unpleasant. The problem is that judgments are made before enough information is gathered to evaluate the situation rationally.

As a little awareness-raising exercise, find a crowded place where people are talking—the office or a party—and just listen to their conversations. See how many ways feelings are expressed. Here are some guidelines to help you stay in the realm of your stress window.

1. Label your feelings: Label them for yourself and label them for others. This is done by simply saying, "I feel angry, frustrated," and so forth.

2. Express your feelings directly to the person concerned: The most effective relief from the stress of unexpressed emotion is to express it to the person or persons associated with it. All too frequently we take our anger out on our friends or spouses.

3. Listen to and allow the other person in the relationship to respond to your communication.

4. Do not use indirect or nonverbal communications to express your emotions: Slamming doors, pouting, refusing to talk, projective labeling, harsh commands, premature judgmental statements are not effective ways to keep interpersonal stress at healthy levels. They increase nonproductive interpersonal tension.

5. Make sure that your nonverbal and verbal communications are the same: Telling someone that you are not angry with them while throwing something

across the room is a double bind. Spend a day looking for double binds in your communication. If you
find them cropping up during communications with
people that are important to you, work on eliminating them. You can do this by expressing your true
feelings directly.

Listening is just as important as talking. Have you ever
seen two people who are angry, both shouting at each other
at the same time? They certainly are not listening to each
other. Their tension stress skyrockets to dangerous levels of
arousal. When that happens, it is a short step to physical
violence. When you listen, put aside your judgments as best
you can. Look at the person's face and listen carefully. Relate your comments to the intention or message of the communication as well as to the emotions being expressed during its delivery. Do not worry about your response until you
have heard the entire message. Do not try to finish what the
other person is saying because you think you know what
he/she is going to say. Communications are important; do
not rush them. They are the regulators of stress in relationships.

10: WORK AND STRESS

Work can be hazardous to your health. First of all, environmental or physical conditions such as noise, temperature, chemicals, and physical demands can increase tension. Second, interpersonal relationships are regulators of stress energy. Finally, your own perceptions are organized into mental-sets that increase or decrease the production to stress energy.

A physical mechanism very important in regulating stress level is the pituitary-adrenal system (see chapter 3). Experiments with animal and human subjects have shown that physical activity and physical stressors affect the activity of the pituitary-adrenal system. Recently, a very important book, *Psychobiology of Stress: A Study of Coping Men*, edited by Holger Ursin, Eivind Baade, and Seymour Levine (1978), has been published that clearly shows that psychological factors dramatically influence the activity of the pituitary-adrenal system in humans. Detailing the physiological and psychological effects of parachute jumping on the human stress response, this book demonstrates that psychological factors (for example, fear of jumping) regulate the activity of the human pituitary-adrenal system. This is one more step in understanding the relationship between stress and disease. It still remains to be proved that stress causes disease, but at least it is known that perceptions and learned emotional responses control powerful hormonal systems that regulate the functions of vital organs and our ability to ward off disease. Clinical and correlational evidence indicates that stress is related to disease. Just exactly how risk factors and stress influence the susceptibility and course of illness is very complex. More experimental data must be gathered to clarify the intricate relationships between stress and disease. There is enough evidence, however, to begin making sensible changes in lifestyle. This is especially true for work. The parachute-jumping studies show, for example, that the stressor of the first jump increases the activity of the pituitary-adrenal system. This results in decreases in the secretion of testosterone, a powerful sex hormone, and increases the level of fatty substances in the blood. Surely stressors encountered during work can drive the pituitary-adrenal system just as effectively as parachute jumping did for Norwegian soldiers.

One study (Frankenhaeuser and Gardell, 1977) examined the activity of the pituitary-adrenal system in relation to different working conditions in a Swedish sawmill. They identified two groups of workers designated as high-risk and control groups. The high-risk group was operationally defined as having work cycles less than one minute. It took less than one minute to complete a single operation, for example, to feed a piece of lumber into a machine. The work was described as physically strenuous, monotonous, and socially isolating. Members of the control group had work cycles of several minutes and more freedom of movement and socialization. As you might have predicted, the high-risk group showed significantly higher pituitary-adrenal activity, as measured by urinalysis, than the control group. The control group also showed a marked decrease in adrenaline and noradrenaline secretion at the end of the workday. They were "coming down" from their day's work. The high-risk group reached their highest levels of secretion at the end of the day. Psychosomatic disorders were also considerable in the high-risk group. All of this strengthens the notion that job stressors are related to disease—possibly bringing on disease or at least aggravating existing conditions. Work can be hazardous to your health, but it need not be.

THE COST OF STRESS TO BUSINESS

Just how much excessive stress and anxiety costs you or the business for which you work is difficult to assess. Some estimates range from 10 to 20 billion dollars for executive tension stress alone. One of the most systematic attempts to estimate the costs of tension stress upon organizations may be found in *Managing Executive Stress: A Systems Approach* by Greenwood and Greenwood (1979). They identify several categories of concern, such as mental and physical illness including depression, accidents, lowered efficiency, turnovers, nonturnover (a problem because unhappy and overstressed workers stay with the organization), and, finally, premature death. Evidence of stress's detrimental effects on workers and production is strong enough to move business decision makers to offer stress seminars and stress-management programs to their workers. Most business leaders view their workers as nonexpendable, a resource to be cared for and developed. Hence they are willing to implement programs to help workers even though there are little data showing the impact on the bottom line —profit or loss.

YOU, YOUR JOB, AND STRESS

It is difficult to put a price tag on the impact of tension stress and anxiety for business. Where stress cost–accuracy may be lacking for the organization, it certainly is not lacking for you. There is one person who can tell you for sure whether your work is taking you down the dangerous road of maladaption. That is, of course, yourself. But even you can be fooled by the tricks of adaptation. You can (and do) adapt to higher and higher levels of tension. It is a gradual process that blurs self-awareness.

Gaining some perspective about how you feel about your work, both physically and psychologically, is helpful. The first step in AIMS, the problem-solving model described in the last chapter, is awareness. Sit down with paper and pencil, describe your physical and psychological reactions, and identify the major stressors of your work. Use the stress-window checklist in chapter 6, to see whether your job stress is optimal. Your score should be close to 50, and if it is over 75, you probably are operating in your stress window. It is absolutely necessary that you occasionally perform a self-awareness evaluation to identify stress reactions and stressors that need managing. As tension increases so does the tendency to deny its effects. Identify problem areas, develop a management program, and self-assess your efforts.

ON BECOMING AND UNBECOMING A WORKAHOLIC

Workaholics are not born that way. They learn to work, work, work. Exactly how and why the compulsion to work to the exclusion of almost all other life activities is learned is not known. There are all kinds of theories—some exotically referring to unconscious desires for a parent of the opposite sex, inadequate oral gratification as a child, and even racially inherited predispositions to produce or create. Although these theories and others are interesting, once you have become a workaholic, the task is to control the work habit. Three general ways to control the compulsion are environmental, temporal, and recreational management. Here are some suggestions based on variations of these management skills to help you control work behaviors and work anxiety.

Environmental management. Only work at the office, or if the office is in your home, make it distinctive from the rest of the house. Bringing work home actually leads to associating home with work. Psychologically this can cut you off from a place to get away from work and relax. By restricting work to the office or a distinctive office in the home, the work environment is clearly differentiated from the home environment. Housekeepers can have a bit of trouble with this suggestion. If you are a housekeeper, you can get around the problem by following the next suggestion.

Temporal management. Schedule your work for specific hours of the day. Failure to clearly identify a time for work and a time for recreation and relaxation can generate anxiety. A good example of this is worrying about work when you are trying to enjoy relaxation or recreation. If you are a housekeeper, you can identify specific times for work. During those times the house becomes a workplace. Outside of those times the house becomes a place for recreation and relaxation. It also helps to wear special clothes while you work and then change them when you are finished. Combining relaxation or recreational activities with work in a home situation often causes feelings of being trapped and, consequently, depression.

Behavioral structuring. Structure your work so that you can easily see that your efforts are productive. Clear definition of work objectives that lead to a larger goal enhances feelings of effectiveness and mastery. This helps develop a perception of generally being in control of your work rather than being controlled by it. See chapter 3 for a discussion of perceived control and behavioral structuring.

Recreational management. Plan recreation and vacations. Give yourself enough time to make arrangements for getting away from work so that you do not have to rush or worry about the job. A participant in a stress-management seminar described his vacation this way: "I begin worrying about a vacation every spring. My wife begins to nag me about going on vacation. We all fight about where we will go. The kids do not want to go where we go. We put it off until the last minute and then the week before is hectic. I work twice as hard at the office to get ready to take a week or two off. I have to make the arrangements tor tickets and lodging. My wife has to get the house cleaned and everything packed. We have to get someone to feed the animals and water the plants. Finally we get there and I am tired and spend the first part of the vacation worrying about not being at work. The second part is worrying about spending too much money and having to go back to work." Frankly, this does not sound like much of a vacation. Taking more time for planning and preparation would help in this case. Part of the preparation should be devoted to getting used to the idea that you will be leaving work for a while. Concentrate on the positive aspects of getting away. Doing that and planning far enough in advance should help you enjoy your vacation more and benefit from the break in work routine. If you need a vacation, try not to combine vacationing with work. A vacation combined with work is often worse than work alone, especially if you are vacationing with family or friends. They will be set for relaxation and recreation. You will be set for work.

ways to deminish

Stress-management programs. Actively manage job stressors and your stress reactions to them by using a stress-management program. There will be some stressors that you cannot change. In these cases, it is necessary to invoke the "acceptance rule." The acceptance rule is a mental strategy that is embodied in the statement "This is, at least at this time, beyond my control. I will accept it and make the best of the situation." This will help you avoid the attempts of overcontrol and overstriving typical of Type A behavior patterns. It will help you forget about work when you are trying to relax.

Learn how to relax. If you know how to relax and can relax after each day's work, then you need not worry so much about stress on the job. A good many of the anxious people who I have seen worry about worrying and the physical tension they experience while working. Energy levels must be tailored to meet the demands placed upon you. Too much or too little energy hampers performance. If your job demands high levels of energy, be sure to learn how to relax, so that you can come down at the end of the day.

WOMEN, WORK, AND STRESS

Excellent studies are beginning to appear in scientific journals which shed some light on how well women are coping with stress in the workplace. It is not that after all these centuries women are finally beginning to work. Quite the contrary, they have been working as hard as or harder than men all along. What is happening, however, is that women are moving into jobs traditionally held by men, for example, they are becoming top executives. They are making decisions that affect the lives and fortunes of thousands of people. For some reason, making corporate decisions in business is supposed to be more important and difficult than making decisions in the home. Corporate decision making also supposedly carries a lethal component that induces psychological and physical disorders in those not made of stronger stuff. Well, that is all nonsense. Decision making and work is decision making and work, no matter who does it or where it is done.

There is no reason why women should have to pay the high price of coronary disease or mental illness just because they are moving into what has been considered "man's" work. Whenever I discuss some of the studies showing differences between male and female stress responses (see chapter 3), I inevitably hear two types of comments, which are often based on misinterpretations of research data or prejudice. One frequently held by those who are critical of women participating equally in the work force is, "Ah ha! I told you so." This means that women are going to have to pay the price that men pay for holding executive positions. The other reaction is one of dismay. Those who favor fuller and fairer participation of women in work are concerned about the predicted costs of stress, for example, increases in heart disease. There are many reasons why both of these reactions are premature:

1. Women seem to have a hormonal advantage that helps them to avoid coronary disease to some degree.

2. Women are not strangers to important decision making and hard work. There is no reason why they should not fare just as well in new jobs as they have in the past.

3. Cultural influences affect women's responses to stressors, but these are learned responses. There is no reason why these learned responses cannot be carried over into the workplace if they are beneficial or changed if they are not.

4. Research on the differences between male and female stress responses is just beginning. It is too soon to draw any valid conclusions about the impact of job stressors on female executives.

Arla Collins and Marianne Frankenhaeuser investigated the stress responses in male and female engineering students (1978). The purpose of their study was to understand to what degree differences in male and female stress responses could be attributed to biological sex differences or to sex-role learning. The subjects were given a cognitive-conflict task in which they were to ignore the meaning of a color-naming word and respond to the color of the print. The word *red,* for example, would be printed in blue ink. The correct response would be *blue.* In addition, incompatible color words were presented aurally just to make the task more difficult. If you want to have some fun with your friends, use some colored pens or pencils to print color names in a color different from the color word. Give them a list of about twenty words and have them identify the color of the print as fast as they can. It is not as easy as it sounds.

Several measures were taken during the experiment. They included heart rate, cortisol secretion, subjective difficulty, adrenaline and noradrenaline levels. Results showed that the pituitary-adrenal secretions of cortisol, adrenaline, and noradrenaline did not differ in the control or relaxation conditions. The control condition established a baseline during relaxation for comparison with the experimental conditions.

Adrenaline production and heart rate increased for both sexes. The rise of adrenaline secretion was greater for males. The rise of heart rate was greater for females. Males showed a significant increase in cortisol production. Females did not. Males reported greater subjective effort in performing the task than females, but there was no difference between male and female task performance.

Part of the reasoning of this study was that earlier findings showing that adrenaline secretion was lower in women than in men but that performance was equal would tend to be reversed if sex-role learning were a more important influence on the stress response than biological sex differences. This would be expected because engineering is a male-dominated course of study and therefore women engineering students should be "culturally" more like males and therefore more similar in pituitary-adrenal secretions. The data tend to support this hypothesis. Pituitary-adrenal secretion differences found between males and females in earlier studies were greater than those of this study where sex-roles were similar. Males still showed higher levels of adrenaline secretion than females, and also greater perceived effort. There were no differences in performance. The conclusion that may be drawn from this study is that social influences, that is, sex-role learning, to some degree regulate pituitary-adrenal system secretions during the stress. Before any other conclusions are drawn more research must be performed.

Speculations about the consequences women will have to face as they begin to claim what has been traditional male territory are legion. Without research data to support them, they remain speculations. It will be many years before we know for sure what the impact of the stress of the business world will be on the health of women. It probably will take as long to determine this impact as it will take for women's salaries to become , on the average, equal to those of men.

STRESS AND THE BOSS

Two important criteria for hiring workers are their intelligence and their experience. A common complaint of younger people is that they were turned down for a job because they lacked experience. Most managers want to hire someone with a high level of intelligence. A recent series of studies (Fiedler, Potter, Zais, and Knowlton, 1979) found some interesting relationships between stress generated to the boss as a stressor and the use of intelligence and experience on the job. Generally a high-stress relationship between the boss and a worker inhibits the use of intelligence. Worker reliance upon experience, however, is enhanced under high stress with the boss. Stressful boss-worker relationships are not necessarily negative.

Sometimes the expectations of the boss enhance perfor-mance. They help generate enough stress energy to move the worker into the stress window. On the other hand, too much stress energy can hamper performance. Furthermore, chronic tension and anxiety over the boss might lead to mental and physical health problems. If the boss-worker relationship is nonstressful, there is a greater tendency for workers to be more creative in generating alternative solu-tions to problems. As stress increases, however, workers fall back on old habits or past experience to solve problems. One adaptive behavior that you can learn to help you use both your intelligence and experience in your job is to mini-mize boss-induced stress if it reaches excessive levels for you. The first step is to assess the impact of your boss as a stressor. If you discover that you experience fear, your hands shake, your heart beats faster, you perspire, or you feel more irritable, then you might try one or more of the relaxation techniques described in chapter 5. You can also use the decision-making model AIMS to help solve prob-lems. That should help you more effectively use your intelli-gence even when your boss-tension is high. If you are the boss, the best bet right now is to create an atmosphere in the workplace that will keep tension between you and your workers at moderate or lower levels. At almost every stress-management seminar I have attended, someone always says, "My boss doesn't have stress problems; [he/she] just creates them in others."

LEARNED HELPLESSNESS, MOTIVATION, AND JOB DISSATISFACTION

Employee motivation, job dissatisfaction, and job satisfac-tion are workhorse topics in management literature. Volumes have been written in an attempt to understand how to motivate employees by increasing their job satisfaction. If you are a manager, how to motivate your employees is probably of interest to you. The concept of learned helplessness is useful in understanding some of the problems of motivation and job dissatisfaction.

Learned helplessness describes the behavioral responses of individuals who because of their experience have learned to perceive that their responses have little or no effect upon the reinforcements or punishments they receive. For example, an employee might think that his or her efforts have gone unnoticed, unrewarded, or that they have been unjustly punished. If that is the case, feelings of helplessness, anger, depression, and a lack of motivation are possible consequences. Offers of additional money or fringe benefits to increase performance or job satisfaction might have little effect on a person exhibiting learned-helplessness behavior. Attempts to motivate employees by assigning new responsibilities or changing job requirements might also fail.

Learned helplessness, then, can lead to a failure of reinforcers most often considered as motivators. Some of the steps useful in restoring the efficacy of reinforcers to increase motivation and enhance performance are the following:

1. Deliver reinforcements or punishments immediately following the target behavior.

2. Whenever possible, clearly identify antecedent events that signal reinforcement or punishment. You can do this verbally prior to delivering the reinforcement by stating exactly what is being reinforced. This helps the employee associate the reinforcement with his/her behavior. It strengthens his/her perceptions of the effectiveness of his/her efforts.

3. Carefully select reinforcers that are perceived as positive consequences. This is often one of the most difficult steps in maintaining desired behaviors. Re-

member that what is a positive reinforcer for one person may not work for another. Try to know the people who work for you well enough to identify powerful reinforcers for each of them.

4. Ensure consistency in administering reinforcements or punishments to all employees. If two people have performed the same task equally well, they should be equally rewarded.

Job satisfaction and stress are generally not serious problems as long as a person perceives that in the long run his or her behaviors are related to the consequences that follow them. This helps combat the anxiety and frustration that comes from feeling helpless or not being in control.

YOUR PHILOSOPHY OF WORK

If work is a dirty word for you, or if you feel that a day's work is something to get through so that you can go home, then you probably will be stressed or anxious. These negative mental-sets produce chronic tension stress and anxiety. If you begin working at the age of twenty-two and work to retirement, you will be working for approximately forty-eight years or 576 work months, or 2,496 work weeks, or 17,520 workdays, or 140,160 work hours—give or take a year or two. That adds up to a full one third of your life during those forty-eight years. In the long run it is important for you to find a job that you like, to use your stress energy to enjoy your relationships with co-workers, and to gain satisfaction from your work. Try to develop a positive attitude toward work by focusing on the positive aspects of your job. Work is stressful. Try to use that stress energy positively.

11: ANXIETY OR ENERGY: IT'S YOUR CHOICE

The next time you are talking with a group of co-workers or friends ask them to name a fear or something that causes anxiety in their life. Usually, you will find a great deal of variety in their responses. What stresses one might not stress another. Even when people share the same stressor, their physical and psychological responses usually differ. The inescapable lesson of this simple exercise is that you learn to respond to certain stressors in certain ways. You are not born with your fears and anxieties. Everyday stress and anxiety can be changed by learning new ways to alter your environment or your response to it. Whether you do or not is a matter of choice. Excluding severe mental or physical disorders, most everyday anxiety and tension can be kept in the realm of your stress window by learning new ways to deal with them. There are, however, some simple solutions that I think harbor hidden dangers.

Antianxiety drugs are useful in emergency situations for short periods of time. It is easy to take a pill for tension. The tension is reduced, but the problem is not solved. Physical side effects usually mar the benefits of the drug. Personal awareness of the need for drugs to reduce anxiety can increase feelings of helplessness. The widespread usage of antianxiety drugs for everyday tension and anxiety is a simple solution with unhealthy consequences.

Simple psychological solutions are as plentiful as prescriptions for antianxiety drugs. All you have to do is just try one certain method and that will solve your problems. The trouble with that is that we are all so very different that no one simple method works for all. What then is the answer to the question, "How can I use the abundant energy produced by the body's stress response as a constructive force?" The answer is not simple nor easily put into action. There is no miracle, overnight cure. But, the following steps are a beginning.

TURNING ANXIETY INTO ENERGY

1. Learn to use a problem-solving model to deal with the events of daily life. The model described in this book is AIMS. I recommend it. It is the most basic and useful method that can be adapted into everyone's unique personality and circumstances. The steps in AIMS are awareness (A); identification of the real problem (I); management of the resources to deal with the problem (M); and self-evaluation (S). Incidentally, if you are saying to yourself that you do not have time to use such a model, watch out! You may be engaging in Type A coronary-prone behavior. Once you learn to use AIMS, it becomes a habit that takes little time. In the long run it saves time.

2. Learn new ways to increase and decrease stress energy. You should select, practice, and learn ways to relax and generate enough stress energy to meet

the demands of the situation. Tension and anxiety occur when too much energy is created, and performance suffers when you generate too little.

Throughout this book I have presented material to help you increase your awareness of your own stress response, to help you identify your stress window, and to help you select methods to use your stress energy as a resource. I have also presented a problem-solving model that works for everyone, individual differences and unique situations included. Now it is your choice whether your stress energy will turn into anxiety and tension or whether you, in the long run, will use it for your benefit. You will not ever get rid of anxiety. It is part of living and growing. But you can keep anxiety from wastefully consuming your stress-energy resources.

GLOSSARY

Acetylcholine: a chemical secreted by nerve cells that enables nerve cells to communicate with one another and to control muscles and glands.

Adaptation: psychological and physical changes that occur within a person in response to changes in the environment. Adaptation can be temporary or long-lasting.

Adaptation Level (AL): a subjective midpoint that emerges when judging the qualities of a number of stimuli. For example, in a series of tones, depending upon the loudness of each tone in the series, one tone cannot be judged as louder or softer than the others. That is the AL. Everything below it is judged as soft; everything above as loud.

Adaptive stress: stress energy that is labeled as pleasant or helpful by the individual and that enhances performance.

Addison's disease: a deficiency in secretion of the adrenal cortex. Symptoms include weakness, loss of weight, low blood pressure, gastrointestinal disturbances, and brownish pigmentation of the skin.

Adjustment: refers to the changes one makes in the environment to increase or decrease his/her stress energy.

Adrenal glands: endocrine glands located near the kidneys. There are two parts: the adrenal medulla, which secretes adrenaline and noradrenaline, and the cortex, which secretes cortisol and other steroids. The adrenals are critical to the stress response and the body's ability to ward off disease.

Adrenocorticotrophic hormone (ACTH): a stress hormone secreted by the anterior pituitary gland. ACTH regulates the secretions of the adrenal cortex. Those secretions help the body ward off disease.

AIMS: stands for an individualized stress-management program consisting of four steps: awareness, identification of the problem, management, and self-evaluation.

Antidepressants: drugs that restore the central nervous system's activity levels to normal and help relieve psychological depression.

Antigen: any substance that produces antibodies in the body. It is involved in allergic reactions and is usually a protein or toxin.

Anxiety: increased physiological arousal accompanied by generalized feelings of concern and worry.

Arousal level: the general level of activity of the nervous system. Higher levels of nervous system activity are related to higher levels of behavioral activity.

Autonomic nervous system: the parts of the peripheral and central nervous systems that regulate the functions of the main organs of the body and the endocrine glands.

Behavioral rehearsal: a stress-reduction technique that involves the use of imagery to work through potentially stressful situations mentally before actually confronting them.

Behavioral structuring: the process of breaking a general goal down into specific behavioral tasks, each of which when completed leads a step closer to achieving the goal.

Classical conditioning: a type of learning in which a response is elicited from the person by presenting a conditioning stimulus. It is then paired with a neutral stimulus. The neutral stimulus will then come to elicit the response. For example, food causes salivation and when a bell is paired with the food, the bell alone will elicit salivation. All autonomic functions such as heart rate, intestine contraction, and blood vessel dilation and contraction can be conditioned.

Cue: any sign, symbol, person, place, or thing that serves as a guide to behavior. A cue may be relevant or nonrelevant.

Desensitization: a learning process that can be used to reduce the power of a stressor. The individual learns to relax in the presence of the stressor.

Depression: a complex psychological and physical condition characterized by feelings of worthlessness, sadness, and helplessness. One type of depression is accompanied by hyperactivity and is called *agitated depression*. Motor depression, on the other hand, involves hypoactivity, a general slowing down of bodily processes and motor behavior.

Double bind: a type of communication in which two contradictory messages are being given. For example, a verbal message of yes might be given with nonverbal signs of no. This creates ambiguity in communication and anxiety.

Endorphins: hormonelike substances produced in the body that are similar to opiates. They help reduce the nervous system response to pain.

Energy-set: a mental attitude that generates an optimal level of stress energy, for example, self-confidence or competency.

Energy-synching: a process by which two people achieve the same relative energy level either by relaxation or generating stress energy.

Habituation: a reduction of nervous system and behavioral responses to repeated presentations of a stimulus.

Imagery technique: a relaxation or stress-energy-generating technique that involves creating mental and sensory impressions of objects, places, and people in the mind. Imagery techniques help individuals control their stress energy to levels appropriate to meet the demands acting upon them at any given time without actually having to confront a given stressor.

Labeling: a perceptual process by which value judgments are assigned to persons, places, situations, or things.

Learned helplessness: a learned perception that the rewards and punishments that one receives are not related to one's behavior or efforts. Chemical changes in the nervous system accompany learned helplessness. These changes are correlated with psychological depression.

Limbic system: a number of brain structures found in the brain stem that are involved in emotion and learning. Many tranquilizers selectively affect limbic system structures to help reduce anxiety.

Major tranquilizers: a group of drugs most frequently used to treat serious mental disorders, that is, the psychoses such as schizophrenia. Chlorpromazine (Thorazine) is an example.

Minor tranquilizers: a group of drugs that are also called antianxiety drugs. They are used to reduce the anxiety of daily living. The therapeutic and side effects of these drugs are not considered to be "minor." Diazepam (Valium) is an example.

Modeling: a type of learning that occurs from observing the behaviors of others. Children learn many of their habits and social behaviors from modeling their parents.

Neurotransmitter: a chemical generally secreted by a nerve cell that when accepted by another nerve cell accounts for the transmission of information from one cell to another. Nerve cells communicate chemically, not electrically. Drugs that affect behavior often do so because they alter neurotransmitter levels.

Nicotine: a chemical (drug) that mimics the effects of the neurotransmitter acetylcholine and therefore is a stimulant.

No-control-set: a mental attitude that one has little or no control over his or her life. The results can be frustration, anger, tension, anxiety, and depression.

Noradrenaline (norepinephrine): a hormone secreted by the adrenal medulla. A decrease in noradrenaline has been correlated with depression. High concentrations of noradrenaline have been correlated with lesions in the coronary arteries. Noradrenaline levels increase as stress increases.

Operant conditioning: a type of learning in which behaviors increase or decrease in probability as a function of the consequences that follow them.

Orienting response: the nervous system and behavioral responses to novel stimuli. The nervous system changes and increases its activity. Orienting behaviors include listening more intently, searching the environment for the source of the stimulus, and increases in stress.

Overcontrol-set: a mental attitude that influences an individual to attempt to control all of the events and people important in his or her life. This type of control is not realistic or possible.

Perceived control-set: a mental attitude of perceiving that one is in control of most of the important aspects of one's life, that one is *not* helpless and therefore can achieve.

Pituitary-adrenal system: the functional relationship between the pituitary, or master gland, and the adrenal glands. Together they secrete the major hormones that control stress, growth, resistance to disease, and sexual functioning. Our expectancies and worries regulate this system.

Reinforcer: any stimulus that follows a behavior and increases the probability of its occurrence.

Relaxation: the achievement and maintenance of physiological and psychological states of calm. Activity in the nervous system changes from a fast activation pattern to a more rhythmic activity. Muscle tone decreases and the body conserves energy.

Risk factor: any condition that is related to a disorder but has not necessarily been shown to cause it, for example, overweight is considered a risk factor for coronary disease. Cigarette smoking is a proved risk factor for coronary disease.

Progressive muscle relaxation exercises: any exercise that involves the successive tensing and/or relaxing of the different muscle groups of the body.

Psychosomatic disorder: conditions where psychological factors aggravate or cause physical disease. These are real disorders and are *not* imagined.

Sensory deprivation: a situation in which sensory stimulation is reduced by placing the individual in a special environment. The nervous system requires some minimal level of stimulation to function adequately.

Stress: the psychophysiological response of an individual to stimulation that is labeled as pleasant or unpleasant by the individual experiencing it.

Stress window: a stress level where physical and psychological performance is optimal. The stress window is different for each of us and depends upon heredity, physical condition, learning, and situational factors.

Synapse: the functional junction between two nerve cells. The nerve cells do not physically touch, but communicate chemically.

Tension stress: a term applied to a level of stress that is perceived as unpleasant by the individual and interferes with performance.

Tranquilizer: a member of a group of drugs that selectively affects the functioning of the central nervous system by altering neurotransmitter concentrations or nerve cell excitability.

Type A behavior: a behavioral pattern often characterized by aggressiveness, striving, hostility, and an exaggerated sense of time urgency. Type A behavior is also called *coronary prone behavior.* Type B behavior is the opposite on the same continuum.

REFERENCES

American Psychiatric Association Diagnostic and Statistical Manual of Mental Disorders. 2d ed. 1968.

Benson, H. *The Relaxation Response.* New York: William Morrow and Co., 1975.

Bommer, M.; Goodgion, G.; Pease, V.P.; and Zmud, R. "Development of an Information System for the Child Abuse and Neglect Service System." *Community Mental Health Journal* 13 (4), 1977, pp. 333–342.

Brady, J. V. "Ulcers in 'Executive' Monkeys." *Scientific American,* October 1958, pp. 95–100.

Capehart, J.; and Pease, V.P. "An Application of Adaptation-Level Theory to Transposition Responses in a Conditional Discrimination." *Psychonomic Science* 10, 1968, pp. 147–148.

Collins, A.; and Frankenhaeuser, M. "Stress Responses in Male and Female Engineering Students." *Journal of Human Stress,* June 1978, pp. 43–48.

Craighead, W. E.; Kazdin, A. E.; and Mahoney, M. J. *Behavior Modification: Principles, Issues, and Applications.* Boston: Houghton Mifflin Co., 1976.

Farquhar, J. "Stress and How to Cope with It." *The Stanford Magazine,* Fall/Winter, 1977, pp. 50–72.

Fiedler, F.; Potter, E.; Zais, M.; and Knowlton, W. "Organizational Stress and the Use and Misuse of Managerial Intelligence and Experience." *Journal of Applied Psychology,* 64, 1979, pp. 635–647.

Frankenhaeuser, M. "Experimental Approaches to the Study of Catecholamines and Emotion." In *Emotions: Their Parameters and Measurement,* edited by L. Levi. New York: Raven Press, 1975.

Frankenhaeuser, M.; and Gardell, B. "Underload and Overload in Working Life: Outline of a Multidisciplinary Approach." *Journal of Human Stress,* 1977.

Frankenhaeuser, M.; and Rissler, A. "Effects of Punishment on Catecholamine Release and Efficiency of Performance." *Psychopharmacologia* 17, 1970, pp. 378–390.

Friedman, M.; and Rosenman, R. H. *Type A Behavior and Your Heart.* New York: Knopf, 1974.

Glass, D. C. *Behavior Patterns, Stress and Coronary Disease.* New York: John Wiley & Sons, 1977.

Glass, D. C.; and Singer, J. E. *Urban Stress.* New York: Academic Press, 1972.

Greenwood, J. W. III.; and Greenwood, J. W. Jr. *Managing Executive Stress, A Systems Approach.* New York: John Wiley & Sons, 1979.

Grenden, J. "Coffee, Tea and You." *The Sciences,* January 1979.

Johansson, G.; and Post, B. "Catecholamine Output of Males and Females Over a One-Year Period." *Acta Physiologica Scandinavia* 92, 1974, pp. 557–565.

Kellam, S. G.; and Schiff, S. K. "Adaptation and Mental Illness in the First-Grade Classrooms of an Urban Community." *Psychiatric Research Reports* 21, 1967, pp. 79–91.

Livingston, L.; and Schrader, C. *Wrinkles, How to Prevent Them, How to Erase Them.* Englewood Cliffs: Prentice-Hall, Inc., 1978.

McClelland, D. C. *Power: The Inner Experience.* New York: Irvington, Halstead-Wiley, 1975.

McDermott, J. F. "Divorce and Its Psychiatric Sequelae in Children." *Archives of General Psychiatry* 23, 1970, pp. 421–427.

Lazarus, R. S. *Psychological Stress and the Coping Process.* New York: McGraw Hill, 1966.

Mason, J. W. "A Review of Psychoendocrine Research on the Pituitary Adrenal Cortical System." *Psychosomatics* 30, 1968, pp. 576–631.

Masters, W.; and Johnson, V. *Human Sexual Response.* Boston: Little, Brown, 1970.

Meichenbaum, D. *Cognitive Behavior Modification.* University Programs Modular Studies, General Learning Press, 1974.

Seligman, M. E. P. *Helplessness.* San Francisco: W. H. Freeman and Co., 1975.

Selye, H. *Stress.* Montreal: Acta, Inc., 1956.

Selye, H. *Stress Without Distress.* New York: McGraw-Hill Book Co., 1975.

Ursin, H.; Baade, E.; and Levine, S., eds. *Psychobiology of Stress: A Study of Coping Men.* New York: Academic Press, 1978.

Wurtman, R. J. "Food for Thought." *The Sciences* 18, 4, 1978, pp. 6–9.

INDEX